THIS BOOK BELONGS TO:

....

MIND YOUR BUSINESS

A Workbook to Grow Your
Creative Passion Into a Full-time Gig

By Ilana Griffo

FOR YOU

Because this book isn't about me, it's about you,
and the goals you're about to crush.

BUT ALSO,

I couldn't do this without my own cheerleaders.
My family, who inspires me, roots for me,
makes me laugh, and feeds me pizza.

Foreword

Everything happens for a reason, I truly believe that. So, it is no coincidence that you are reading this right now. Seriously, everything has happened in your life—missing the bus, taking an internship, choosing a college or choosing to not go to college, picking up this book—to bring you to this moment. Reading this page.

For years I dreamed of owning my own business. In fact, I would fill notebooks with ideas and bore friends at dinner parties talking about everything in my head. But it was all talk, no action. There wasn't a guide or book or lesson to help me make those dreams reality. Sure, there were business books, but they were BORING. Nothing spoke to me. And so I worked in a job I didn't love because I didn't know where to start or where to turn.

Fast forward to the present: I'm the Founder and CEO of not one, but *three* successful businesses. And as a female business owner, I'm especially proud to own a million-dollar business (meaning I've reached over one million dollars in revenue in a year), something that only 2% of female business owners do! I'm most known for creating Unique Markets, the largest indoor pop-up marketplaces in the country, back in 2008 when the economy was in rough shape. No one thought thousands and thousands of people would want to pay an entrance fee to shop locally and support independent designers and artists—except me. From that very first marketplace in December of 2008 to now, the company has always been in the black.

Since starting the markets, I've helped to rejuvenate the American economy by getting people to shop locally and I've worked with almost

10,000 small business owners across the country. I've spoken about innovation and creativity in retail at conferences such as SXSW, Girlboss Rally, and Create & Cultivate. I've won awards and have been featured in my favorite magazines. In fact, I was on the cover of one! I turned my dream of being a business owner into a reality through hard work, grit, struggle, and many failures. This is why I am so impressed with Ilana's book. Finally, here is a book that can help you create a roadmap! Literally.

This book will inspire and educate, and it uniquely pairs actual exercises and assignments so that you are present and interacting. Instead of simply telling you what to do, Ilana has curated moments throughout the book to help you put pen-to-paper to actually develop your idea. You'll answer questions such as, "Why do I want to start a business?" You'll understand what obstacles are in your way, and how to surpass them. She'll help you figure out when to start, what pages should be on your website, and how to find your community.

Reading this book and working through the exercises and assignments will help you to answer so many questions. You will flesh out your ideas and take one giant step closer to being a boss!

My best advice to hopeful and inspiring entrepreneurs has always been "You just need to start!" Put one foot in front of the other—even when you're not sure there is ground underneath—and you'll reach your goals. This book is a giant step forward. I'm excited for you and your big idea!

Sonja Rasula
Founder & CEO of Unique Markets

Introduction

Have you dreamed of starting your own business?
Perhaps you have already started a side gig and you're ready to take your talent to the next level. It's intimidating, right? You know your craft, but the thought of running a business seems overwhelming.

I get it. I've been there, too. I've been through everything you're experiencing—and I'm still going through it! In 2011, I designed and launched my stationery line, *Sugar & Type*. It included a day planner and a series of cards; I created these items in the evenings and weekends as a way to keep my creative juices flowing when my mundane day job left me feeling less than inspired. The sacrificed sleep was worth it: I left my full-time job as an art director in 2015 and grew my business into a six-figure design studio. I love story-telling, organized rule-breaking, and impactful design. My professional identity is "designer," but I'm also an expert in hustling to launch and grow creative businesses. I love inspiring people to do what they're good at. Every day, I get to help my clients develop their own brands. It's a dream come true.

When I started my own business, I had questions. So. Many. Questions. Sometimes mentors helped me to find answers; sometimes I sent brave emails; other times I relied on my dear friend, Google™. I learned through trial and error. There was a lot of blood, sweat, and tears. I still have questions (all the time!) but I have learned so much along the way.

Millennials have been referred to as "serial entrepreneurs." More than half of us either plan to start our own businesses or already have. We are willing to take risks, eager to build something of our own, and we've got SKILLZ. We want to create our own version of the American dream: we're passionate, multi-talented Jacks and Jills of all trades. But, the practical skills required to launch and start a business aren't necessarily taught in school.

My motivation to write this book is simple: I want to help you kick some major ass in your creative endeavor. I want you to feel empowered as a business person *and* as a creative. I want you to embrace the "business side" of your work. This book is not your mama's business plan. *Mind Your Business* is written for creative souls who want to grow their passion into something more. If you dream of building a business doing what you love—whether it's a full-time gig or a side hustle—this book is for you.

A friendly heads-up: there are no shortcuts, no magic potions, and no get rich quick schemes in this book. Success and good things take time. This book is here to help. I've based everything written here on my experience and what I've learned through my network. There are always circumstances that might not apply to you, but take all that you CAN from this book and run with it! Haters, put this book down and see ya later. We're all just a work in progress. You'll come back to this book over and over as you grow, change, and learn. Take this framework and tweak it to make it truly yours.

Mind Your Business is written in a workbook style, designed to help you get organized with actionable steps to achieve your dreams. It's a book for list lovers, creative spirits, and go-getters. This book can be your business-owner training wheels—a sidekick, reference, guidebook, and the fuel for your creative journey.

I'm here with you every step of the way. Connect with me on social media @ilanagriffo and #mindyourbizbook. You've got this!

CHAPTER 1

Big Picture

Here we are. You're ready to start your own business. (Or you're at least ready to *think* about starting your own business.) Either way, this is a very exciting time! This first chapter guides you through important first steps: you will clearly articulate why you want to start a business, assess your own strengths and weaknesses, identify obstacles and opportunities, and more—all to lay a strong foundation for your new venture. Let's get started!

DOWN TO BUSINESS

Let's get right down to business: working for yourself is uncertain, but so is every other job! Being your own boss can be the most rewarding, exhausting, and fulfilling job you'll ever have. While the idea of starting your own business may seem daunting, cast aside those vulnerabilities for a hot sec. Believe me when I say that you can absolutely do this.

I started my business in 2011. Technically, I'd been freelancing for a while, but mostly to save up for things I needed in college—like a legit copy of Adobe® Creative Suite®. I started a blog and called it *Sugar & Type* because, well, I love dessert, and . . . I'm obsessed with typography. No joke, I can't go a day without either, so that's what I wrote about. The economy sucked, and I couldn't find a decent job doing what I wanted when I graduated. I took whatever freelance job I could find, made contacts at all of the local agencies, and, no shame, even got a job at the mall. Every freelance job I took taught me a little more about working for myself. I learned as much about what I *didn't* want my career to look like as I learned about what I *did* want it to look like. I worked for trade, I worked for minimum wage, I took on every project I could find to get experience. When I finally landed a job in my field, I came home at night and designed some more. Those sleepless nights paid off: my business grew, and once I left my full-time job, I never looked back.

While this book title references growing your creative passion into a full-time gig, I don't want you to think that's what defines success. You may decide you love doing your thing part-time, as a side-hustle, or to fund your passion for travel. You may really love your full-time job (and the health benefits), and that's great! You'll find what works best for you as you make your way through the chapters.

If you're stuck at a job you don't love, stop wasting your time and energy complaining about it. Instead, think of it as a gift: that job is paying you to be able to grow your own business. Use your lunch break to develop your business, schedule in time for your loved ones, and then hustle hard in-between. There's no magic formula. It's a lot of hard work. Your business is your new life. Your hobby. Your obsession.

This book isn't for the dreamers, it's for the doers. It will help you start on your journey to growing your creative passion into something more. Document your ups and downs and every bit of the scary, exciting, wonderful ride of being your own boss. Don't worry about what you don't know or about your terrible handwriting. Just make a mark. This book has your back.

WHERE DO I START

I might as well start this book with a cliché. Screw it, let's start with multiple clichés! It's scary to get started—but it's way easier than putting things off. They say that if you do what you love, you'll never work a day in your life. It's a lie. You'll work all the time, but it'll be worth it!

So where do you start? Start . . . somewhere! Make a project, do a thing, take a photo! We learn best by doing, so get your feet wet. Don't overthink things. Don't quit your day job just yet; remember that good things take time.

**Starting somewhere now
is better than starting somewhere later.**

You'll never know until you try!

Some things take time.

You may not be there yet. But you're closer than yesterday.

**Stop being afraid of what could go wrong
and think of what could go right.**

Doubt is a dream killer.

Make it happen!

FUEL YOUR PASSION

Working for yourself is risky—there's no arguing that. There's no guaranteed paycheck, and no one contributing to your 401K or health insurance. It's daunting, to say the least.

However, if you are passionate about sharing your talents with the world and you're ready to put in the work, the reward is tenfold. You can do what fills you with joy, make a living, and thrive. You're in charge and you can design your ideal life.

Here's the thing: you can't half-ass this. Your passion deserves your attention. You owe it to yourself. We spend so much time working; imagine a life where you LOVE what you do.

Now, the path to where you want to go is NOT going to be easy, especially when you already have so much on your plate. Perhaps you're in school, or working a full-time job, or maybe you have three kids at home. But you're passionate and you can do this! You'll be devoting nights, weekends, and lunch breaks to pursuing your dreams, but you're willing to put up with some shit to attain them. You'll lose sleep and eat meals at your desk, but you're going to love the process. You're climbing a mountain and the views along the way are going to be as important as the view from the top.

You're a creative and you're suiting up to be a smart businessperson. As an entrepreneur, you're wired to dream bigger, work smarter, think differently. Your work can be hard—and enjoyable, productive, and rewarding. From here on out, you're going to do something every day that gets you closer to your goal.

Give yourself credit for the knowledge and experience you already have under your belt. A job—even one you don't particularly like—still offers opportunities to soak up experience and knowledge, and may even be a way to save to launch the business of your dreams.

And about "side projects." Let us never refer to these with quotation marks again. They're important—really important. I constantly work on passion projects. Simply because I love what I'm working on, these projects make my portfolio shine and they can lead to the types of other projects that I dream about at night.

You're about to live and breathe your dream. With passion and with proper planning and execution, you're going to achieve amazing things!

DO IT WITH PASSION OR NOT *at all*

WHY DO I WANT TO START A BUSINESS?

Here's your chance to define your WHY. List the reasons you want to start your own business. (If "passion" isn't one of your reasons, this book might not be for you!)

- To do what I love
- To work for myself
-
-
-
-
-
-
-
-
-
-
-
-
-

MAD LIB-ERATION

At the end of the day, you're the only one who can keep yourself accountable for crushing it in your business. Create a mantra for yourself to help you kick ass and crush your goals.

I AM A _____. I AM READY TO LIVE MY

LIFE. I AM A TALENTED _____. I WILL PUT UP WITH

_____ TO GET TO MY DREAMS. I KNOW IT WON'T BE EASY

AND _____ BUT IT WILL BE WORTH IT. I WILL VALUE MY

TIME AND MY _____. I AM READY TO PUT IN THE

TIME. I WILL LIVE, BREATHE, AND_____ MY

BUSINESS. I WILL DO _____ THINGS THAT SCARE

ME DAILY. I WILL VALUE MY LOVED ONES SUPPORT AND

THEIR _____ I WILL REMEMBER THAT I AM

LUCKY TO BE ABLE TO _____

_____.

Share your mantra on social media
#MINDYOURBIZBOOK

DEFINING SUCCESS

One of the beautiful things about building your own business is that YOU get to define what success looks like. Remember, this is all on your terms! What is important to you? At the end of the day, what will it take for you to feel successful? How does this differ from conventional definitions of success?

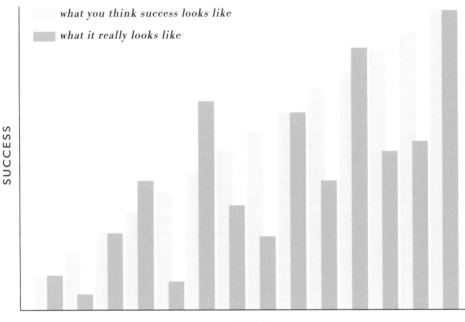

what you think success looks like

what it really looks like

SUCCESS

TIME

Definitions differ, but "success" is usually messier than it appears on the surface! The things that are important to you—your values—should inform your goals. Not what the Internet says or what someone else wants. Revisit your personal definition of success from time to time to make sure it still aligns with the work you're doing. What does success look like to you?

I THINK 'SUCCESS' IS ME approving OF ME WHICH FEELS LIKE IT'S GOING TO BE A LIFELONG THING.

JEN GOTCH

CHIEF CREATIVE OFFICER | BANDO.COM | @JENGOTCH

GET TO KNOW YOURSELF

It can be difficult to objectively identify your own strengths and weaknesses and to assess your own communication style. There are a variety of personality tests (search online!) that can help you get to know yourself and how you work.

WHAT ARE MY STRENGTHS?

WHAT DO I NEED TO OVERCOME?

WHAT DISTRACTS ME?

WHAT'S MY SPECIAL TALENT? WHAT DO I DO BEST?

Let's hope you find "self-motivated, attention to detail, determined, and time management" on your list. If not, I suggest that you work to develop those traits or find a business partner or employee to help fill in the gaps.

WORKING FOR YOURSELF

Being your own boss is not for everyone. Pause to consider the many aspects of owning your business and what your day-to-day work life will look like.

PRO	CON
Pants optional	*No watercooler chats*

CURRENT RESPONSIBILITIES

It's useful to assess your current responsibilities and commitments. Doing so will help you to determine how much time, treasure, and talent you are able to devote to building your new business.

- *Student loan payments*
-
-
-
-
-
-
-
-
-
-
-
-
-

WHAT'S STOPPING YOU?

A main character in a rom-com might dramatically quit her job, throwing all caution to the wind. In real life, careful planning is usually the better approach. You'll never feel totally ready, but you can do your best to plan and prepare. Use this page to help clearly define what, how, and when you'll be ready to set out on your own. *(Hint: Feeling nervous is good. It shows you're aware of risk. You'll never be 100% ready, through, so let's aim for 99% and move forward!)*

I want to have _____ saved up to cover my ass.

I want to accomplish _____ before I leave my job.

I need enough money to purchase _____.

I'll leave my job on _____.

I got laid off from _____, and it's fuel to my fire!

I can't find a job in my field of _____, so I'm starting now!

NOTES

....

....

....

....

....

OBSTACLES

It can feel like there are a million obstacles to overcome when you're starting a business. Some of these are very real (money, materials) and some of them live only in your head.

So what's stopping you? Do you feel like an impostor? If so, let's kick that thought in the butt! You don't need a certain number of hours or a specific level of experience to be credible and valuable. Position yourself as an expert and act like one. Your talent and your tenacity will be your driving forces. If there are areas in which you need to improve, there are plenty of resources to help you.

I also recommend that you consider what worst-case scenario may be if things don't work out the way you want them to. In fact, being prepared for a variety of outcomes is good business sense.

OBSTACLE	REAL	IMAGINARY
	☐	☐
	☐	☐
	☐	☐
	☐	☐
	☐	☐
	☐	☐
	☐	☐
	☐	☐
	☐	☐

TRY SITES LIKE LYNDA.COM® OR SKILLSHARE.COM®
TO BRIDGE ANY SKILL GAPS YOU MAY HAVE.

SUPPLIES

Starting your own business is particularly humbling when you realize you don't own a stapler. You may be transitioning from an office with a well-stocked supply closet. Make a list of the supplies you will need to get started and build a budget for these supplies based on estimated costs. You can start to save for the big-ticket items.

SUPPLIES   **COST**

AM I WILLING TO INVEST
my time and money?

(circle one)

YES   NO

GREAT! Let's celebrate!

If you answered "NO", let's dig deeper, and find out WHY. My guess is that you THINK you don't have the money to get started. (If you're lazy, I'd suggest putting this book down and waiting until you're ready to dive in.) If money is a concern (and when isn't it?) there may be other options to consider.

Are you in a position to ask for investors?   ☐ **YES**   ☐ **NO**
Can you scale back and start small?   ☐ **YES**   ☐ **NO**

Carefully research potential investors. Consider making a show-stopping video and launching a campaign on a crowd-funding website.

Then, tell EVERYONE you know about your project. Get a little vulnerable and reach out to people you think will be interested. Use your village (your family and friends) and ask them to help spread the word!

RECOMMENDED READING: *THE $100 STARTUP* BY CHRIS GUILLEBEAU

WHEN TO START

Timing is everything, they say. There's some truth to that notion. A great idea at the wrong time may lead to frustration. Of course, there's never a "perfect" time to take a leap, but use this page to help you discern if you should pursue your idea now or if you need to pump the brakes. List your reasons below. Which column has more reasons listed?

NOW   OR   WAIT

FEEDBACK

Share your business idea with your friends. Talk to people and gauge their reactions. Get real, honest feedback about your new venture. Record what you learn here:

NAME　　　　　　　　　　　　　**DATE**

FEEDBACK

NAME　　　　　　　　　　　　　**DATE**

FEEDBACK

NAME　　　　　　　　　　　　　**DATE**

FEEDBACK

IMPROVE

How can you improve your idea using the feedback you have received?
Don't hesitate to incorporate feedback and pivot when necessary!

THE CREATIVE PROCESS

oh yeah

IDEA!

UH-OH DOWNWARD SPIRAL

internet WORMHOLE

BINGE EATING

THIS IS OK!

PROGRESS

how will I top this?

WHAT'S NEXT?

BOSS BEWARE

IMPOSTOR SYNDROME - Impostor Syndrome is real and EVERYONE feels it. Remind yourself that it's normal and okay to feel this way—and then say, "Screw it! I got this!" It's fine to be scared. It's proof that you're passionate. Let it be fuel for your hustle! You are not alone—stop comparing yourself to strangers on the Internet.

Use the space below to write words of encouragement for yourself, things to remember when you experience low points. You have to become your own biggest fan, even if it doesn't come naturally to you. If you've got a little "perfectionist" in you (or a lot), it's time to get over it. Perfection is not achievable, but you'll always be growing, learning, and improving.

INTROVERTS - It's your job to sell yourself, to show others that you possess talent and offer value. If you are reserved and not used to reaching out to others, this can be uncomfortable at first—but it's critical. Schedule a practice phone call with a friend and use that time to polish your pitch. You'll soon be ready to reach out to potential clients!

NAME   **DATE**

NOTES

RECIPE FOR SUCCESS

BE AN EXPERT - If you don't consider yourself an expert, how will others? Lean into what makes you unique. Own your quirky style, your weirdness. Your experience and approach to your work makes what you offer special. Constantly remind yourself WHY you're chasing your dreams and work to project what you want to be known for. If you're just starting out or haven't yet created a project you want to share, FAKE IT! Devote time to a personal project to showcase the type of work you want to attract. Don't wait for opportunities, make them! Document your process and share your work, even if you don't think it's good enough. Remember: if you wait until it's perfect, you'll be waiting forever.

SHOW UP EVERYDAY - Are you ready to show up everyday (and nights and weekends)? You need to be willing to put in time and work. Make a schedule: slate time for clients and time to work on your business. (And no, these are not the same thing.) Be reliable: people need to know when they'll hear from you. Stay relevant: be eager to learn and grow. Find your rhythm. This will take awhile, and that's okay! Make sure you're ready to commit. You are your business. If you don't show up for your business, no one else will.

GET COMFORTABLE WITH SELF-DOUBT - Self-doubt is going to become your new neighbor. It's going to pop in all the time. I'm telling you now: it's normal. It's okay. Don't let it rain on your parade of awesome. You CAN do this, and I'm rooting for you!

SCALE UP - You want to build a business that's going to last. Consider if what you're building is sustainable and has the ability to grow. Can you hire employees as needed? Are you prepared to outsource? Set boundaries (you'll break and reset them!) and be prepared with a game plan.

POSITION yourself AS AN EXPERT & ACT LIKE ONE

BUSINESS ROADMAP

What do you want your business road map to look like? I revisit my "road map" yearly (sometimes more) to make sure it still feels right, adjusting as needed. Remember: it's not set in stone.

Goals

....

....

....

6 MONTHS

3 YEARS

Goals

....

....

....

You'll find yourself setting, breaking, and reestablishing boundaries and goals throughout the life of your business. There are no right answers when it comes to finding your creative path.

1 YEAR

Goals

_____

_____

_____

Goals

_____

_____

_____

5 YEARS

Vision Board

Close your eyes and take a moment to revel in your vision of what you want your business to be. Dream big. Hold onto this vision; use this space to cut and paste images or words that inspire you.

final thoughts

NOTES and TAKEAWAYS

You finished the first chapter, and that's a BIG deal. Pop the champagne! (And no, it's definitely not too early to celebrate.) You have done so much more than just read a few pages. You have taken major steps toward taking your dreams—and yourself—seriously. You have articulated your goals and started on the path toward your dream. Congratulate yourself!

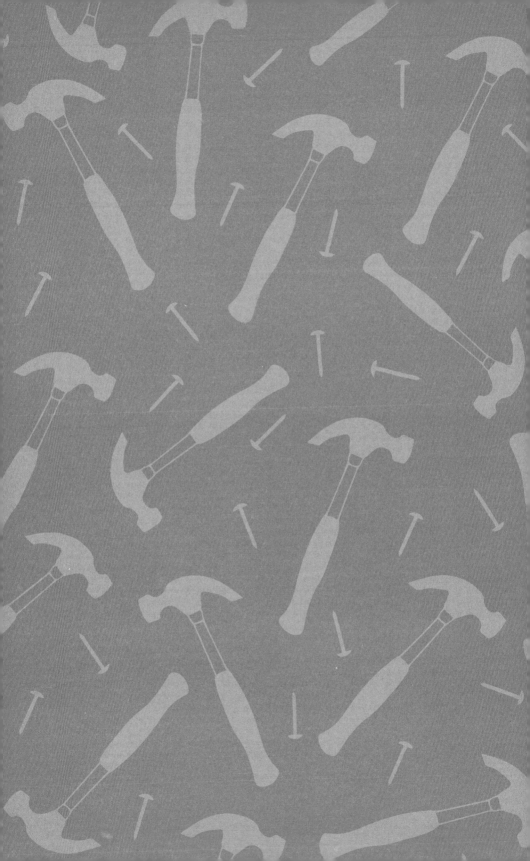

CHAPTER 2

Building a Brand

Close your eyes and envision the business you want to build. Can you see yourself happily collaborating with clients or picture your products displayed in your favorite boutique? Building a strong brand identity is an important part of bringing the image in your head to life. This can take a lot of time and thought. Lucky you, this chapter will help you on your way. Here we go!

BRANDING 101

Many people first think of logos when they hear the term "branding." But branding is so much more than that! Branding is also about the experience someone has with your brand—how they learn about your business, the way they feel when they interact with your business, and how they think and feel following their interaction. Branding involves the look and feel of your business card, the colors you choose, and even the tone of your voice in videos or blog posts. Your identity includes the style and colors, and your logo is an actual mark that's consistently used for recognition.

You must employ a consistent brand voice to create a memorable brand experience for your clients and customers. Consider your core values (see exercise on page 49). These values will inform how you bring your brand to life—how it aligns with who you are as a business owner and how you are unique in the market. From your social media posts to your product packaging and everything in between, you should strive to create a cohesive brand experience that reflects the values and beliefs that drive your business.

WHY DO YOU FEEL DRIVEN TO DO WHAT YOU DO?

WHAT VALUES INFLUENCE YOUR BUSINESS? HOW?

ICING ON THE CAKE

Here's a great way to think about branding: it's everything clients hear, see, and feel about your company. Without a strong foundation, the beautiful logo and color palette won't hold up. My friend Kelsey Kerslake of *Pinegate Road* said "No amount of cake decorating is going to make the cake taste better." She hit the nail on the head here. As a fan of cake, I love this analogy to illustrate how while frosting is delicious, it's best when eaten atop a really delicious cake.

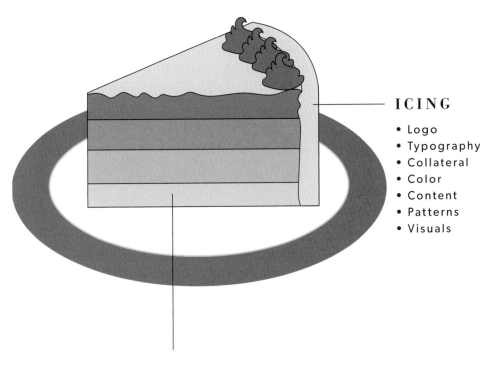

ICING

- Logo
- Typography
- Collateral
- Color
- Content
- Patterns
- Visuals

CAKE

- Your "Why"
- Your Client Experience
- Your Brand Strategy
- Social Media Presence

WHAT'S IN A NAME

Of course, one of the first points of order is to name your business. Coming up with a business name can be really hard. Start by brainstorming a list of words you might associate with your business. Once you have your list, try pairing different words together. You should try for something that is easy to pronounce, meaningful to your brand, and available (make sure someone else doesn't have it!). It's fine to use your own name if you are comfortable doing so and if this makes sense for your business structure and future.

-
-
-
-
-
-
-
-
-
-
-
-
-

NOW IS BETTER *than* LATER

ALL ABOUT YOU

Maybe you still don't know how to pronounce "niche" (hey, neither do I!) but it's important to know what it means. If you are specializing in 25 different services, how can what you offer really be special? Specialization should be, well, special! Figure out what attracts people to your work.

For my own business, the words "playful," "typographic," and "crisp" come to mind. My ideal clients love puppies, the outdoors, and dessert. (They're basically me!) However, when I first started out, I took every job I could land. This helped me to figure out which projects I really enjoyed, what my strengths were, and—just as valuable—where I struggled. This knowledge was crucial in helping me to define my business. Now I know exactly what projects light my fire and the type of client I work well with.

Your unique style has a huge impact on the types of projects and customers you attract. You know you can't be everything to everyone, so don't try! I want to know what attracts people to your work. What makes your work special? Why do people want to work with YOU? The ability to articulate this is one of the first steps in defining your brand.

WHAT LIGHTS YOU UP

WHAT BRINGS YOU DOWN

CORE VALUES

To build a successful brand, you have to start with your values. WHY are you chasing this dream? What gets you out of bed in the morning? Are you trying to help people? Maybe you want to teach people to bring more joy into their lives through your work. This exercise can be really hard, but it's important. Don't skip it!

WHY

HOW

WHAT

BEING CREATIVE is an opportunity to try new things. Trust your gut and take creative chances. But honestly, everyone is just making it up as they go. That's the fun part! If your values are your starting point, your work will be intentional and meaningful.

FIGURING IT OUT
AS YOU GO

GETTING IT RIGHT
THE FIRST TIME

WHAT AM I doing AND WHY?

ELEVATOR SPEECH

It's important to be able to clearly articulate what you do as a creative. You have probably had some awkward encounters with people who think your work is just a hobby. Let's fix that. Use this space to craft your "elevator speech," a clear, succinct explanation of what you do and why. Revisit this page as you work through this book and revise your elevator speech as needed. When someone asks you what you do, you will dazzle them with your poise and passion rather than tripping over your words. Trust me, an effective elevator speech is an element of your brand (even if it's somewhat indirect).

TARGET MARKET

You should craft your message to target your dream client. Who is your target audience? Learn as much as you can about them. What are their struggles and pain points? What excites them? The more you learn, the better you'll discover where and how to get in front of your dream client.

The following chart will help you to identify characteristics and preferences of people in your target market. While not every client will fit the same mold, this exercise gives you a way to begin to identify your niche. Once you have a clear sense of your primary market, you can make important decisions with them in mind.

Ask yourself what value you have to offer. What do you have in common with your "ideal" customers? Where do your passions overlap? How can you create content that will appeal to them?

YOUR IDEAL CUSTOMER

AGE :

GENDER :

LOCATION :

MARITAL STATUS :

CHILDREN :

EDUCATION :

INCOME :

DREAM VACATION :

SELF CARE ACT :

HOBBY :

SPLURGES ON :

SAVES FOR :

FAVORITE BRANDS :

CELEBRITY SPOKESPERSON :

BRUNCH OR HAPPY HOUR :

VALUES :

CATS OR DOGS :

COFFEE OR TEA :

CITY OR COUNTRY :

SALTY OR SWEET :

TWITTER® OR INSTAGRAM® :

BEACH OR MOUNTAINS :

FICTION OR NON-FICTION :

CHOCOLATE OR VANILLA :

BRAND BUZZ

Identify buzzwords that you can use time and time again as another way to build brand consistency and your brand voice. For example, do you use "ladies," "gals," or "women" when you speak to your audience? Rather than creating an artificial voice, think about words that you use naturally. Brainstorm buzzwords that relate to your values and your brand:

....

....

....

....

....

WHAT VIBE DO I WANT TO COMMUNICATE WITH MY BRAND?

WILL THIS SPEAK TO MY AUDIENCE? If your target market is looking for something high-end and you're DIY-ing everything, you're not aligning with what your target audience wants. Even though *you* like something, double check to make sure your audience will like it too. Building a brand is all about the people you're serving.

Your Vibe Attracts Your Tribe

BRANDING ELEMENTS

SUBMARKS - Your logo needs to work both large and small. Introducing a secondary mark provides a unique brand system that works in multiple sizes and formats. Secondary logos, monograms, and badges are all effective tools to enhance your brand. For example, a photographer's logo (usually their name) is too hard to read when it's small. A secondary mark with their initials or icon can be used as another asset, such as a watermark or wax seal for packaging.

ORIGINAL ART - I hope this goes without saying, but copying is wrong. Use something original. It can be simple, but it must be unique.

SLOGAN / TAGLINE - A slogan or tagline explains what you do and the impact you make with just a few words.

HIERARCHY - What's the most important word (or words) in your business name? *(Hint: words like "to" and "the" are seldom going to be most important.)* Hierarchy is a design term that refers to using scale and other elements to emphasize a particular word or words, drawing in the eye.

LEGIBILITY - Duh. It needs to be legible! How will people find you if they can't read or pronounce your business name?

COLOR - Use color, by all means, but don't be overly reliant on it. Your logo should not rely on color alone to be striking. One or two colors is more than sufficient for most logos.

CONSISTENCY - Brand recognition requires consistency. From the colors you use to the tone of voice you use in your social media or marketing materials, consistency is crucial to establish and solidify your brand, making it recognizable. One of the fun parts of branding is creating unified collateral that helps tell your story through every interaction your clients have. Business cards, social media content, blog graphics, packaging, templates, presentations, and so much more—these are all pieces of the puzzle that make up your brand.

YOUR BRAND VIBE

Ideally, your brand should attract like-minded individuals. Your purpose, passion, interests, voice, and style all create a brand culture to attract customers. A personality-infused brand has a human element that makes people feel they can relate—and it makes them want to work with you! Remember that your brand aesthetic encompasses so much more than type, color, and messaging—it is also about a human connection.

As a designer, you might expect me to preach "Hire a designer!" right away. As a business owner, however, I understand that it's not in everyone's budget from the get-go. I'm all about asking a design student or a friend to help you out for a reasonable price, as long as you've seen their portfolio and think their work fits your style.

You want a versatile mark that fits your needs and reflects your core values. This might be your business name, beautifully typeset in a classic style. Start with something simple and clear, and save up the funds to invest in a professionally-designed brand identity when you're ready for a refresh down the road.

Legibility is the most important concern as you select typefaces. Try to anticipate what scale the fonts will be viewed at and what feelings you want them to convey. Do you want something modern or classic? Perhaps you like a hand-drawn look, or you may prefer a clean, streamlined aesthetic.

Think about selecting brand colors. I recommend that you choose one or two colors to incorporate in creative ways (tissue paper, packaging, etc.). Don't simply pick the color of the year. Rather, make sure the color aligns with your values and what will appeal to your audience. (Hello, color theory!) You can certainly have a larger color palette, but focus on one or two main colors and use the others as accents to add flavor.

The brand board on the following page features elements important to the look and feel of your brand. Whether you develop your brand yourself or work with a professional, use this chart as a reference for the necessary elements to develop.

BRAND BOARD

PRIMARY LOGO

SECONDARY LOGO

COLOR PALETTE

TYPOGRAPHY

PRIMARY TYPEFACE

GIBSON REGULAR
abcdefghijklmnopqrstuvwxyz
ABCDEFGHIJKLMNOPQRSTUVWXYZ
0123456789

SECONDARY TYPEFACE

BODONI URW OBLIQUE
abcdefghijklmnopqrstuvwxy
ABCDEFGHIJKLMNOPQRSTUVWXYZ
0123456789

PATTERNS

COLLATERAL

Your brand isn't just about the look of your business—but the look and all those little details sure are exciting! Brainstorm ways—big and small—that you can go above and beyond with your branding. Consider it this way: every package you ship and every email you send is an element of the brand experience. Each piece can either fall below, meet, or exceed expectations. Which of these do you want for your business? Those extra details all create brand recognition, from the on-brand gold foil (everywhere!) to the sticker you place on outgoing orders. Consistency allows people to spot your work from a mile away (or in a pile of mail waiting when they get home from work!).

Personalized thank you gifts

Branded Stationery

YOUR WEB PRESENCE

Building a website can feel like a huge hurdle, but really, it can be quite simple! I recommend a few platforms based on different needs. Use this flow chart to identify your ideal platform, then use your network to find someone with great style who can help you customize to fit your brand.

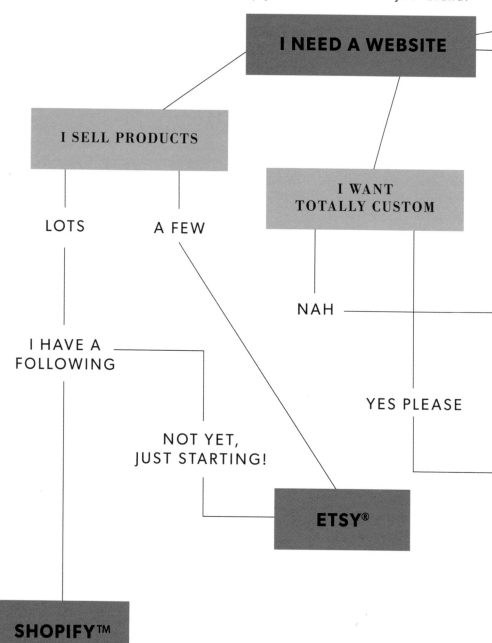

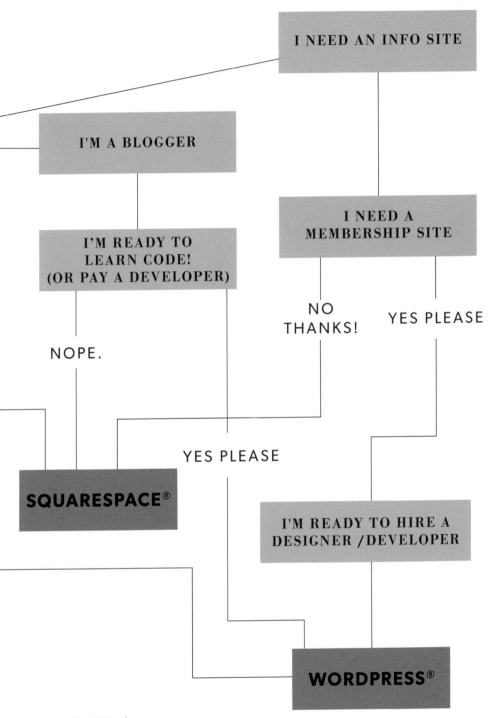

I NEED AN INFO SITE

I'M A BLOGGER

I NEED A MEMBERSHIP SITE

I'M READY TO LEARN CODE! (OR PAY A DEVELOPER)

NO THANKS!

YES PLEASE

NOPE.

YES PLEASE

SQUARESPACE®

I'M READY TO HIRE A DESIGNER /DEVELOPER

WORDPRESS®

DISCLAIMER | There are plenty of other website platforms you can use; I have found those on this page to be user-friendly, reliable, and of high quality.

WEB DESIGN

There are many elements that need to be written and built to create a great customer or client experience on your website. Who will visit your site? How long will they stay? How will they access your site (phone/tablet/computer)? Is e-commerce necessary? Do you plan to blog? With so many things to think about, I highly recommend that you work with a web designer and developer. For you ambitious creatures who find HTML and CSS exciting, dive in! There are many great platforms that provide a foundation you can customize; many of these platforms have tutorials to help you get started. Begin by drawing a very basic framework and take one page at a time. Be sure to list all the information you want on your site. Carefully craft the copy to reflect your core values to your audience. *(Hint: if writing isn't your forte, it's a good idea to think about working with a copywriter. After all, your website is an important point of interaction with potential customers.)*

If you plan to tackle building your own website, use this page to map out thumbnails of your site. You can also use this space to help you determine what information you need to gather (photos, copy, etc.).

HOME

ABOUT

SERVICES

PORTFOLIO

SHOP

CONTACT

SITE MAP

A site map helps you envision the flow of your website and how visitors will experience it from one page to another. In the chart below, use the top row to list your main navigation. The remaining boxes are for secondary pages reached from the main navigation. This tool will help you establish your website hierarchy and make sure it's easy to move from page to page. You may need more boxes or fewer, but this guide will get you started.

Make sure to explain who you are, what you do, and provide contact information. The latter can be a contact form or a hyperlinked email address. Link to your social media platforms. Finally, it's important to include copyright information on your site.

DOMAIN NAME:

final thoughts

NOTES and TAKEAWAYS

You finished the second chapter and your business is taking shape. You look GOOD! Whether you created a look that serves you right now or worked with a designer to develop something with staying power, you're making moves in the right direction. Reward yourself: put that new logo to use and order a customized mug, phone case, or even a sticker for your car!

CHAPTER 3

Marketing Magic

When it's effective, marketing definitely *feels* magical! However it's mostly a lot of hard work—research, analyzing your competition, building a following, and so much more. It's all about how to tell your unique story to the people who will want to hear it. Easy, right? The following chapter will lead you through some valuable exercises to craft your marketing message—and the magic is sure to follow!

MARKET RESEARCH

Just as it's important to know your audience, it's equally important to research and analyze your competition. You can learn a lot by trying to understand what works well for other successful businesses.

WHAT MAKES MY PRODUCTS OR SERVICES SPECIAL OR UNIQUE?

WHAT'S MY MISSION STATEMENT?

WHO ARE MY COMPETITORS?

WHAT ARE CURRENT TRENDS IN MY MARKET/INDUSTRY?

WHAT DO MY COMPETITORS CHARGE? DOES THIS VARY?

WHAT IS MY PRIMARY MARKET? SECONDARY MARKET?

HOW CAN I EXPAND MY MARKET?

CUSTOMER EXPERIENCE

One of my favorite exercises is to storyboard services and the corresponding client experience and then test it on people. You can get really creative here! The client experience impacts how you will be remembered. It's important to establish rapport and trust with clients.

The storyboard below is inspired by a photographer friend of mine. Read on to learn about her carefully crafted killer customer experience!

1 | *Potential client researches "wedding photographers" in their city. Since the photographer has devoted time to SEO, producing new content, and getting reviews, her site pops up on the first page. The same occurs when searching a local wedding hashtag on Instagram.*

2 | *The client lands on the photographer's website and is drawn to the beautiful images and well-designed layout. The client recognizes a few people in the images. Using the website contact form, the client sends an email to inquire about pricing and availability.*

3 | *The client receives a prompt reply; the email thanks the client for reaching out and offers congratulations for the upcoming event (a wedding!). The client is also provided with a link to the photographer's calendar and is invited to schedule an appointment. Finally, the photographer includes a welcome kit with additional photos to browse and key points about her philosophy and her unique approach to wedding photography.*

4 | *The client books an appointment and immediately receives a confirmation email. This well-designed and informative email thanks the client for making an appointment and explains what to expect at the upcoming meeting.*

5 | *On the day of the appointment, the engaged couple is greeted with bubbly in branded flutes and warmly welcomed into a lovely studio. The photographer's consultative approach and enthusiasm seals the deal, and the couple can't wait to book. They leave with a sweet treat—a chocolate bar with the photographer's logo on the wrapper)—and a feeling of assurance that they are in good hands.*

6 | *The wedding day is incredible; the photos that capture the special event are delivered in a timely manner, along with a lovely bottle of champagne, a USB customized with the photographer's logo, and a coupon for their next session.*

7 | *The relationship between the photographer and clients continues for years. The couple receives an anniversary card every year and they continue to book sessions with the photographer to capture milestones at different life stages.*

Use these boxes to map the experience you want YOUR customers to have.

ATTRACTING NEW CLIENTS

THE NEW COLD CALL - Put yourself out there! If you see someone you want to work with, start by engaging with them on social media. Comment on their posts, make sure they're a good candidate, and see if they could benefit from working with you. Build a relationship and tell them about what you do. Consider requesting a video call to talk about what each of you does; this may lead to a conversation about how you can work together. Before the call, be sure to have your elevator pitch down cold and your services list right in front of you so that you are prepared to answer questions without fumbling. You don't have to be sales-y, but you should have a genuine interest in what they do and how you could work together. It may turn into a sale, a referral, or just a nice conversation.

FAKE IT 'TIL YOU MAKE IT - Devote time to create your dream projects. If you're a designer and you want to do branding and web design for people in the fitness world, you need to have relevant work samples in your portfolio. It makes no difference if it's a real project; it's still a way to show potential clients what you can do!

Brainstorm people to contact and get your work in front of:

NAME   **CONTACT INFO**

RETURNING CUSTOMERS

It's easier (and cheaper) to work with returning customers than it is to attract new ones, so it pays to keep your existing clients happy. There are many ways to stay engaged with your past and current clients to keep them coming back for more. You DON'T want to hard sell every time you talk with a client, but you do want to keep in touch and on their radar.

If you see something in the news or on social media that makes you think of a client, reach out and tell them. Follow your clients on social media and comment on their posts. Send a branded gift or a handwritten note if there's an appropriate opportunity. Clients who are impressed and happy will speak highly of your work and refer others to you. That, my friends, is free marketing at its finest!

Birthday cards

Repeat customer incentives/discounts

OUTREACH

Whether you're just starting out or you've been at this for years, you always need new clients. You MUST talk about what you're doing—scream it from the social media rooftop, tell your friends, and ask your family to do some bragging on your behalf. If you are a product shop, consider doing a pop-up at a local boutique. If you're a nutritionist, host a workshop at a local gym or leave promotional material at the front desk. If your clients are virtual, do some research to find their physical addresses and send some good, old-fashioned snail mail (beautifully designed, of course)!

Some people scoff when they think about outreach, worrying that it seems desperate. I disagree. I believe it shows that you're passionate, that you are willing to proactively reach out to people you think are a good fit for you and your business. When you are professional and put your clients' interests front and center, outreach feels positive and authentic.

When I was about to graduate from design school, I made a list of all the places I wanted to work. I researched and found the names of the art directors at these companies and compiled the information in a spreadsheet. Then, I made a series of letterpress mini-prints and mailed one a day for four days. On the final day, I included a note with my website and a statement about why I wanted to work for the company; I also let the art director know that I would call the following week. *(Hint: it worked!)*

PROMO & OUTREACH IDEAS

GET CONNECTED

Another really great way to get clients? Word of mouth! Hear about a new product from a trusted friend? Boom. Add to cart. It's your job to start telling people about your product. Talk confidently about your services! Make a social media account so people can follow what you're working on.

SPREAD THE WORD - Make it fun! Host giveaways with your products. Offer a discount code. Collaborate with someone who has a similar following and offer something that fans will really want. This will all remind people what you're up to and even help you find new faces. Remember, people can't hire you or buy from you if they don't know what you're doing. Get your work in front of people!

TRENDING - What's going on in the world? What's trending and does it tie into your business? Food bloggers can ride the wave of "National Ice Cream Day"; photographers can offer "fall mini sessions" just in time to catch the leaves changing color. Use "Throwback Thursday" to feature an old project or "Motivation Monday" to inspire your followers.

GET INVOLVED - Find a professional organization in your field of work and get those referral networks going. Jump in on conversations in your field on social media platforms.

MAKE FRIENDS - Form relationships with other creatives; you can talk about your successes and struggles and offer support to each other.

FIND YOUR FAN CLUB - Find people who support you: friend, family, clients, and customers. Be good to them.

Brainstorm other ways to get connected:

TOO MANY IDEAS

If you've got the fire of an entrepreneur, you likely have a million ideas for projects and ways to grow your business. However, if something only makes you money but doesn't fill your cup, it's probably not worth pursuing. The ideas that light your fire and support you financially are the ones that will truly fulfill you. Whatever you're considering—creating an online course, designing digital downloads, or anything else—make sure it aligns with your big picture goals before you dive in.

IDEA	DO IT FOR THE LOVE	DO IT FOR THE MONEY
	☐	☐
	☐	☐
	☐	☐
	☐	☐
	☐	☐
	☐	☐
	☐	☐
	☐	☐
	☐	☐
	☐	☐
	☐	☐
	☐	☐
	☐	☐

Ask for WHAT YOU want

SOCIAL MEDIA

Building relationships and attempting outreach through social media is powerful, but it's also a BEAST. Consider your audience and figure out which platform they're hanging out on. (You might be surprised to know that people still build incredible, trending, successful businesses using Facebook®!)

CROSS-PROMOTE - If you blog, make sure you also share your content on Pinterest®. If you feature a special offer on Instagram, you should also send it to your email list and Twitter followers. Just be sure to tweak the content for each platform.

REAL TIME - In my opinion, it doesn't matter if you post in real time or are a #latergram fan. I prefer to use Instagram stories for real-time updates and my feed for planned, curated content. There are plenty of great apps to help you schedule your content in advance. Experiment and find what works for you.

ENGAGE & PLAN-ISH - You don't have to publish every day, but you have to be engaged. Respond to comments, reply to questions. Follow other people that inspire you and get active on their feeds! You never know what wonderful ideas and friendships can spark. Use your editorial calendar to plan what you want to share so you're always prepared to post something.

GET PERSONAL (OR NOT) - On a platform like Instagram that's all about visual interest, it's great to show a styled photo. But also think about showing behind the scenes: the dirt, the chaos, what it takes to really create that perfect image. It's a chance to be vulnerable and connect on a different level. On the other hand, if you don't want to share pictures of your kids or home life on your business page, then don't! Do what works for you, just be consistent and keep your focus on your WHY. I prefer to have one account where I can post it all; that works for me right now.

STOP COUNTING FOLLOWERS - Don't measure your success in followers. I mean it! I know it's easier said than done. A loyal following doesn't have a size requirement. Sure, your ego might get a boost from seeing a "K" next to your Instagram account, but does it change your value?

USE HASHTAGS - Use hashtags. Tag accounts that relate and may want to feature you. Tag sources. What do you have to lose?

KEYWORDS & SEO

Honestly, what is SEO? And how the heck do you use it? It's one of those things that we hear about, but it's difficult to explain. SEO stands for **S**earch **E**ngine **O**ptimization. Basically, it's how people can easily find you online. Keywords are used in product descriptions, captions, and behind the scenes of your website. Using them effectively makes your content easier to find. Think about it: you obviously want to be one of the first listings that pops up for your category when someone searches online. Unfortunately, it's not simple. Organic growth is wonderful, but a little SEO doesn't hurt. If you want to take things to the next level, there are plenty of courses you can take or experts you can hire to work the SEO unicorn.

For the sake of stating the obvious, you want to create **sharable content.** (Duh, right?) Study the social media accounts you admire and figure out what makes something trend. For example, a trending recipe on Pinterest will usually have a drool-worthy photo AND include the recipe name. On Instagram, a video shot from overhead allows people to see how easy it is to make a recipe.

Keywords matter. Use Google Ads™ Keyword Planner to find keywords that are highly relevant for the content you're creating. If you don't know your market well, you won't know what type of keywords to use! A little research goes a long way. On Etsy, search similar and popular items and note the words they are tagged with. On Instagram, search hashtags and record the ones that are popular for your audience. You get the idea. Jot down keyword ideas here:

KEYWORD IDEAS   ### HASHTAG IDEAS

....

....

....

....

WORDPRESS® USERS: CHECK OUT THE "YOAST® SEO" PLUGIN

ENGAGEMENT

I've said it before, but it's worth repeating: never judge someone's success by their (or your own!) Instagram follower count. True, the more people who see your product, the better the chance that someone will buy it. At the end of the day, though, engagement is what matters. A modest following with solid engagement is where it's at! Use the space below to brainstorm ways you can engage on social media. Brainstorm ways to engage on social media:

- Give something away for free
- Pose questions to followers
- Start a challenge or hashtag
-
-
-
-
-
-
-
-
-
-

DON'T measure SUCCESS -IN- FOLLOWERS

EMAIL MARKETING

We spend a lot of time in our email inboxes and we WANT to pop into someone else's! While social media is a great way to grow a following, with changing algorithms and new platforms constantly popping up, it should be a priority to land your business in someone else's email. After all, when someone opts-in to your email list, they give you permission to share with them. Your email list is like a VIP party: those who sign up get to be the first to know about important news and updates for your business.

Make your email communication relevant and worth the time to read it! You're in control of how often you contact people on your list; it's a good idea to establish a clear goal for an email campaign and effective strategies to reach your goal.

WHAT DO I PLAN TO SEND VIA EMAIL? HOW OFTEN?

WHO AM I EMAILING? DO I NEED TO BUILD DIFFERENT GROUPS FOR TARGETED MESSAGING? WHAT ARE THESE GROUPS?

FREE STUFF

Everyone loves free shit—that's no secret! I'm all about a coupon, a good deal, and great value. A quick way to gain trust, grow a loyal following, and keep people excited and engaged is to give something away for free. Hopefully, people will love what you are offering so much that they'll stick around and eventually become a paying customer!

Creating an opt-in is essential to grow your email list. Make a way for people to sign up in the header on your website, in your email signature, and in your Instagram bio.

If you are offering advice and tips to your industry, it may feel as though you're teaching your competitors your secrets. Really, though, it's YOU that makes your brand unique—your voice, your messaging. That's something you can never give away. Here's the rule of thumb to follow: give something away, but keep something to sell.

FREEBIE IDEAS:
- Free training, e-book, or printable download
- Free item with purchase or a 25% off coupon

Brainstorm creative opt-in ideas:

MAILCHIMP AND CONVERTKIT ARE TWO EMAIL MARKETING PROGRAMS I SUGGEST YOU LOOK INTO. SEE WHICH ONE MEETS YOUR NEEDS!

EDITORIAL CALENDAR

Use an editorial calendar to plan the content you will create and share. For example, in November and December, your posts might be geared toward holiday content, the services you offer that make great gifts, or some of your favorite gift ideas (either your own products or products of your friends in the industry). Use this page to brainstorm content ideas and use the next few pages to plan when to publish them. Don't forget to consider that people shop for gifts weeks before the holidays, and if there's a DIY involved, they need even more time. Don't be afraid to re-share something you worked on the previous year, too! How about a round-up of your favorite holiday projects from years past? Know what you're going to publish ahead of time and have your content in queue and ready to go.

-
-
-
-
-
-
-
-
-
-
-
-

JANUARY

FEBRUARY

MARCH

APRIL

MAY

JUNE

JULY

AUGUST

SEPTEMBER

OCTOBER

NOVEMBER

DECEMBER

TIME IS SLOW FOR THOSE WHO WAIT

Reference your editorial calendar and develop a social media calendar for an entire month. This exercise will give you a good sense of the amount of time and brain power you need to devote each month to plan and produce quality content for your social media channels.

SUNDAY	MONDAY	TUESDAY	WEDNESDAY

Don't forget: you don't always need brand new content. Share a project from last season or do a round-up of things you've already created. Plan ahead to ensure you always have something to share and ways to engage your followers.

THURSDAY	FRIDAY	SATURDAY	NOTES

TACTICS AND STRATEGIES

Marketing is the way you communicate your brand. From your business cards to your email newsletters to your Instagram posts, it's all marketing! There's a difference between marketing strategies and marketing tactics. Strategies are big, broad concepts that apply as a whole. Tactics are more specific and relate to the way you use your strategies on specific platforms. The key to effective marketing is to set a goal and then develop a strategy and tactics to help you get there. With your goal as the starting point, work backward to plan all the necessary steps to achieve it.

WHAT IS MY GOAL?

_____

_____

_____

WHAT STRATEGY CAN I USE TO GET THERE?

_____

_____

_____

WHAT TACTICS WILL HELP ME MEET MY GOAL?

- _____

- _____

- _____

- _____

- _____

if you want to WORK FOR *yourself* YOU HAVE TO MAKE YOUR *own* OPPORTUNITIES

JEN AND AMY HOOD

final thoughts

NOTES and TAKEAWAYS

You made it through this chapter; you've been busy! A deep understanding of your target audience is essential to the ultimate success of your business, as is a solid, well-developed plan. You have learned about how to engage with your market and how to cater your content to your target audience. You're on the same page as your dream clients and you know the best way to communicate with them. You're ready to deliver the goods to your fans. Go get 'em!

CHAPTER 4

Find Your People

I'll give it to you straight: it can be really hard to go at it alone. Being a small business owner can be lonely. And scary. Of course, creating your own business from the ground up is incredibly rewarding—but it's important to acknowledge the challenges.

This chapter is all about building up community and systems to support you when the going gets rough (and it will). Your people are out there— people who are experiencing many of the same things you're going through, people who want to see you thrive. Let's find them!

MENTORS

Nobody gets by without a little help. I'm not implying that you need a business partner, but you definitely need support. That support can come in the form of tools, systems, or mentors. I've had many mentor relationships along the way: teachers, colleagues, parents, and friends (both virtual and IRL).

Twitter is an amazing way to interact with your industry heroes. Get on their radar and examine how they tell their brand story through social media. This may open doors to build a mentor relationship.

Identify six people you want to reach out to. Take time to learn about them. Comment and engage on social media. When you email, make it personal! Do they mention how much they love a local donut shop? Ask if you can buy them a donut there! If they're not local, offer to buy a virtual coffee for their time. Make sure to check if they offer paid coaching sessions; if they do, sign up for a session! Their time and resources are valuable (just like yours!), and be sure to respect that. If things don't work out, move on (and don't take it personally). You don't have to have a formal conversation to ask someone to be your mentor, but a relationship that *feels* like a mentorship can begin to form.

Who do you plan to reach out to?

1.

2.

3.

4.

5.

6.

IF YOU'RE A DESIGNER, AIGA HAS A GREAT MENTORSHIP PROGRAM! BE SURE TO CHECK OUT YOUR LOCAL CHAPTER AT WWW.AIGA.ORG.

SCORE.ORG/FINDAMENTOR IS A GREAT RESOURCE. YOUR LOCAL CHAPTER CAN HELP TO CONNECT YOU WITH A BUSINESS MENTOR.

LET THE beginner LIVE ALONGSIDE THE expert

JEN SINCERO

AUTHOR & COACH | JENSINCERO.COM | @JENSINCERO

COFFEE DATES

Jot down five people to grab coffee with. Local peers are a great resource and can help combat the loneliness that often comes with working by yourself. You want to build a relationship, hopefully one that will benefit both of you. Reach out and offer to buy someone coffee because you love their work!

1

NAME

EMAIL

NOTES

2

NAME

EMAIL

NOTES

3

NAME

EMAIL

NOTES

4

NAME

EMAIL

NOTES

5

NAME

EMAIL

NOTES

RESOURCES

Asking for production resources and pricing information can be sensitive subjects, and what works for one person may not be what you need. Make sure you value the time of the person whose expertise you're tapping; understand that no two businesses are exactly alike and that finding the right resources takes time. There's a lot of trial and error. The right paper for me isn't necessarily the right paper for you. Some people want to keep their resources proprietary, and that's okay. Don't waste their time asking questions that you should already have researched—show that you're working hard. For example, "Do you have the name of a printer?" is a question I get all the time.

Instead, make sure you've researched the type of printer you need and come with a more specific question such as, "I've been looking for a printer that does matte gold foil on recycled paper for my customer's business cards. Do you have any resources or a place you recommend looking for samples? I've tried XYZ, but the price was too high." Getting specific demonstrates that you're serious, that you actually did the work, and that you understand and appreciate the time, skill, and experience behind any recommendation you might receive.

When you do have the opportunity to meet with someone in your field, make sure you're prepared with specific questions related to the work that person has done. In other words, open-ended question such as "How do I get clients?" might not be the best use of time. Whenever I receive a comment or question asking for advice via social media or email, I feel honored that someone values my opinion, but I 'm aware of the fine line between answering a question and consulting on business advice.

When you're stuck, tap the resources you have come to rely on: your favorite teacher, Google, online forums, podcasts, books, friends, mentors, and so on.

List the resources you need—an invoicing system, for example—and brainstorm ways to find them:

ONLINE COMMUNITIES

Community over competition! When we support each other, great things happen. Facebook groups are an amazing place to find community— people who share your same struggles and fears. It's also a great place to find referrals, job postings, and get feedback on your work. Be sure to review group rules before posting!

BEING BOSS - Also a podcast, this group is for creative entrepreneurs and is all about owning who you are and making things happen.

CREATIVE LADY COLLECTIVE - A supportive community for female creatives that offers networking, feedback, support, and encouragement.

THE IMPERFECT BOSS - A growing movement on a mission to make imperfect normal and inspire women to be real and confident in life and work.

THE RISING TIDE SOCIETY - Educates and empowers creative entrepreneurs to thrive in the spirit of community over competition. Look for a local chapter and a "Tuesdays Together" event in your city.

THINK CREATIVE COLLECTIVE - Helps creative entrepreneurs develop systems to build profitable and sustainable businesses. The founders also have a podcast and offer courses.

SAVVY BUSINESS OWNERS - Where female entrepreneurs create, connect, communicate, and collaborate.

Can't find a community that focuses on your industry? Make one! Pop into other groups, see what they're all about, and then create your own group for YOUR people!

MASTERMINDS - There's no doubt you've got a running list of people in your industry whom you admire. Maybe you've connected a few times through social media or email. Those people are GOLD. Schedule a recurring video call where you can discuss struggles, celebrate accomplishments, and feed off each other's energy. I'm currently in two of these "Mastermind" groups, and each time we talk someone has an "aha" moment. First coined by author Napoleon Hill, these Mastermind calls spark so many great conversations. From pricing to hiring help, we bounce ideas and learn from each other every time. You can also start a Slack® Channel, the modern day AIM®.

IRL COMMUNITY

Find your tribe and love them hard. Make a note of your personal and professional A-team: family members, your bestie, your significant other, an industry friend who's a few steps ahead. The cruise director, the backup dancers, your most supportive bra. Who has your back?!

Many cities and states offer resources to support small business owners and entrepreneurs. Check government websites or do an online search. You might be surprised at what's available!

LIST YOUR A-TEAM:

....

....

....

....

Grow your circle and you're bound to meet people who can introduce you to your dream clients. You never know who knows who, and the more people you can connect with, the more opportunities you'll find! Go to local networking events or invite a few people to start a local group. Look for local organizations to join; this is a great way to meet people and seek advice.

AIGA - An amazing resource for graphic designers. Be sure to check out your local chapter.

SCORE - The nation's largest network of volunteers offering free small business advice.

....

....

....

....

....

final thoughts

NOTES and TAKEAWAYS

We get by with a ton of help from our friends! When you work for yourself, it is so important to develop a community of like-minded business owners. Water those friendships like they're a trendy little fiddle leaf fig. (Are you even supposed to water those?) Don't be afraid to ask for help when you need it. Make connections, both virtually and IRL (in real life).

CHAPTER 5

Scary Stuff

Early in this book, I talked about how you can fake it 'til you make it. You can be whatever you want to be, do whatever you want to do. Obviously, you should be qualified to work in your chosen field. (You probably can't be a graphic designer if you haven't ever used design software.) Assuming you have all the necessary know-how, there is still a load of things you need to do to "legitimize" your business. The following chapter is all about the "scary" parts of being a business owner—choosing a business entity, protecting your work with copyright, protecting your ass(ets) with a solid contract, and more. Here's the thing: it's not that scary. I promise. Let's walk through it together.

SPAGHETTI NUMBER

What's the minimum amount you need to make each month if you eat spaghetti every day? Figure out your bare minimum income requirement by writing down all of your expenses per month. I heard about the "spaghetti number" from *The Lively Show*, episode 8 with Kim Vargo of *Yellow Brick Home*, and I've been using it since! Use these pages to help create a budget.

EXPENSES	PLANNED	ACTUAL (BE HONEST!)
Me (treat yo self)		
Rent		
Phone Bill		
Insurance		
Cable		
Other Utilities		
Savings		
Groceries		
Gas / Transportation		
Loans		
Charitable Donations		
Memberships		
Entertainment		
Misc. Expenses		
TOTAL EXPENDITURES		

SPENDING LOG

Write down everything you'll purchase throughout one month. Consider if it's benefiting your business and goals, or if it's something you simply want to have. Getting checks from clients is exciting, but don't blow it all on things that won't help you to achieve your goals. Creating a plan will set you up for success, and you'll be able to treat yourself too!

DATE	$	DESCRIPTION
TOTAL		

BUSINESS EXPENSES

EXPENSES	SPENT
Website Domain	
Website Hosting	
Advertising	
Hiring Help *Developer, Contractor*	
Rent (if needed)	
Insurance	
Memberships	
Cost of Goods	
Accounting Service	
Taxes	
Supplies	
Software	
Mileage	
TOTAL EXPENDITURES	

BIZ OVERHEAD

Everyone's "oh sh*t" fund is different. This is an account that you can fall back on if you need to. What if your furnace breaks during your first month of business or your car breaks down six months in? Think about what you need to be comfortable and what you need to survive.

Use your budget planner to determine the minimum amount of money you need to earn each month. I suggest having enough money to cover at least six months of expenses in case you aren't able to bring money in. Remember that your work can ebb and flow if you're a freelancer, so some months will be slower than others. Keep an eye on your expenses while you're adjusting, and start small. You still have to pay to keep your business running, even if things are slow. Consider your worst-case scenario and plan for it. I left my job when it started to get in the way of my freelance work, and I was confident because we had an emergency account in case we needed it. I decided I'd try freelancing for one year before throwing in the towel.

SLOW MONTHS & LULLS - When you work for yourself, you have to know that your paycheck won't be consistent. You might bring in 25% of your annual income in one month; the next month, you might barely break even. During slow months, I like to work on personal projects, take online classes, try something new to broaden my skill set, and create passive income projects. Don't use a slow period as an excuse to sit around and do nothing. Instead, blog, practice, experiment, and learn! Use the time to look up from your work and seek inspiration. Use the space below to brainstorm projects you can do during slow times:

REVENUE STREAMS

Brainstorm seven different revenue streams you can establish. You won't build them all at once; begin with one or two and slowly add on over time. (Most millionaires have seven income streams, so let's take a cue from them!)

1

2

3

4

5

6

7

YOU *deserve* EVERYTHING YOU *want* BUT YOU HAVE TO WORK *really* F*CKING *hard*

SONJA RASULA

ENTREPRENEUR & BADASS | SONJARASULA.COM | @SONJARASULA

PRICING

Many people feel uncomfortable and awkward talking about money. Strive to feel confident about the prices you establish for your services or products. You know your value. Your pricing should be informed by a number of factors: your experience level, your time, the market, and location. Your time and your talent have value and it's your job to educate your clients on what that looks like. At the beginning, you'll "pay your dues" and work for less than you'd like (or maybe even free) while you're soaking up experience like a sponge, but it's not forever.

Take the time to carefully research the going rates in your field. If you sell products, identify similar products and businesses and analyze what they charge for goods like those you plan to sell. If you offer services, sites like Glassdoor.com might yield useful information about going rates in your field.

Ultimately, what you charge needs to sustain both your personal needs and your business expenses. It's useful to do some old-fashioned number crunching. What is your goal salary? To determine this, begin with your monthly income requirement as a base. Reference the "spaghetti number" and spending log you calculated early in this chapter. Think about your monthly business expenses. Once you know your target salary, work backward to see if your pricing and the number of projects you typically work on each month will enable you to realistically meet your goal. Make sure your goal reflects your time, value, the demand for what you do, and that it is in line with your industry.

CRUNCH THE NUMBERS

Know your WORTH THEN ADD SHIPPING FEES taxes PROCESSING and CONTRIBUTIONS TO YOUR retirement

PRICING

ROI - It's also important to calculate your ROI percentage ("Return on Investment") as you price your goods and services. Here's a simple formula to help you out:

$$\text{MATH!} \quad \frac{\textbf{BENEFIT } (profit)}{\substack{\textbf{INVESTMENT MADE} \\ (cost\ of\ goods,\ labor,\ overhead,\ etc.)}} \times 100$$

If you offer services, know that different pricing structures may be appropriate for different types of clients and projects. Consider establishing a variety of pricing structures, including:

FLAT FEE - Your contract should clearly outline the services and parameters your flat fee covers. Clients might experience some sticker shock when presented with a flat fee, so it can be beneficial to present different levels of service. Empower your client to make the choice that best suits their budget. If your client asks you to do more, you can kindly point them to your contract—remind them you're available to amend the contract to include additional work for an additional cost.

HOURLY RATE - Contract work can be billed hourly. Don't forget to factor in taxes, supplies, and health insurance, just like a "regular" job would! Creative projects can be difficult to price hourly because the impact isn't always comparable to the hours logged. Update your hourly clients on your time and progress as you work so they can plan accordingly.

DAY RATE - You should determine how much you charge for a day of work. What supplies will you need if someone hires you for a day? Estimate travel time, transportation costs, and any other factors that might influence your day rate.

MINIMUM PROJECT FEE - With experience, you'll figure out if a project isn't worth your time. One or two large projects may be better than twenty small-time clients. Set a "minimum project fee." You can say no to projects that don't meet your established minimum.

RUSH FEES - You're not a robot and you can't always churn out work on demand. Set a time frame that you consider a "rush" job. Is it 24 hours? One week? It's acceptable to tack on a rush fee for something that requires you to drop everything else or change your plans to work over the weekend.

Pricing isn't one size fits all. Consider each client or project individually bearing in mind these factors:

CLIENT PROFILE - Think about the client and the "reach" of the project. You should charge more for a large corporate client with a project that will be viewed by thousands than you should for a local mom and pop shop.

AUDIENCE - Who will view what you create? How many views? What is the demographic of your target viewer?

USAGE - Is the project a one-time poster design or is a logo that will be used across a variety of marketing materials for years to come?

COPYRIGHT AND OWNERSHIP - Who owns the artwork you create? Does the client own the work or do you retain rights? The client may also request to license your work for a limited time or for limited use.

Once you've done your research and considered the relevant factors, you should feel confident in the pricing you establish. However, there is still an art to discussing pricing options with potential clients. Here are some things to think about as you sit down with your potential clients:

ASK FOR A BUDGET - It's perfectly acceptable to ask someone their budget range. Often, clients won't even know what to expect; it's your job to educate them on your value and industry standards.

SIGN A CONTRACT - Do not—under any circumstances—start any work without a signed contract and a deposit.

BE FLEXIBLE - If a client says they can't afford you, think about how you can work within their budget. Is there a service you can eliminate, or somehow change the scope? Can you offer a payment plan spread over six months? You can present tiered pricing options to show value added with additional services. Remember: it's up to you to sell clients on what you have to offer.

Pricing strategy involves a ton of factors, many of which can shift over time. Demand can ebb and flow. Perhaps you receive feedback that your pricing is too high (or too low!). Be willing to periodically evaluate your pricing and adjust as necessary. Strive to reach the right people and to convincingly explain your value.

PRICING INDEX

I just threw a lot of information your way. Use this page to reflect on what you have learned and how it applies to your business. This can be a useful reference tool as you book jobs and work on your business finances.

MONTHLY COST OF DOING BUSINESS

MONTHLY BUDGET

FLAT FEE

HOURLY RATE

DAY RATE

RUSH FEE CHARGES

CONTRACT TEMPLATE DRAFTED?   ☐ YES   ☐ NO

NOTES:

BUSINESS MODELS

It can be confusing to determine what type of legal entity is appropriate for your business. Consider the tax implications, impact on income, and potential liability for each of the options below. Each state (and country) has different laws, so be sure to research the appropriate laws and guidelines for where you live and talk with your lawyer and CPA.

SOLE PROPRIETORSHIP

YAY
- Register your business locally
- Inexpensive to create
- No federal government requirements
- No crazy legal documents to file
- No one else to split profits with
- Taxes are uncomplicated
- Easy to discontinue

NAY
- Owner is liable for business debt
- Creditors can force the sale of proprietor's personal assets
- Company debt is owner's debt
- Limited access to capital (no partner)
- Ends if owner retires or dies

PARTNERSHIP

Two or more people who co-own a business for the purpose of making a profit. The law doesn't require a partnership agreement, but you should have one.

YAY
- Easy & inexpensive to form
- More money to start
- Complementary skills

NAY
- Difficult to find a partner with the same vision, priorities, and willingness to invest time and money

S-CORP

An S-Corp passes all net income through individual shareholders. This avoids double taxation and is beneficial for startup companies.

LLC

In a limited liability corporation, the owners are not personally responsible for debts and obligations; your personal assets are protected. Rather, the business is responsible, only business assets are vulnerable (unlike in a sole proprietorship).

TOO LEGIT TO QUIT

You know your craft and you've got that special something that only you can offer the world. There's no certificate that tells you that you can start a business, but there are a few legal steps, to help you run a "legit" business.

DBA - Stands for "Doing Business As". Setting up DBA (unless you're using your own name) is a great step! First, check with your state about the regulations and requirements. You'll need to pay a filing fee, typically between $10 and $50. It's an easy form and you can celebrate with bubbly afterward. You can also set up a DBA if you have a corporation but want to do business under multiple names (shorter names, perhaps). Corporations are state entities, so you'll need to talk to the Department of State for any information regarding your DBA.

EIN - An EIN is an Employee Identification Number. This is for the federal government. This number is assigned to a business entity, sort of like a social security number. If you're a Sole Proprietorship, you do not need to file for an EIN, but you certainly can. You can use it on forms from clients (like a W-9) instead of sharing your social security number. This helps to keep your business separate and professional. You'll need your EIN for taxes and for banking. You can get more information at apply for an EIN online at **irs.gov/business.**

STATE TAX ID - Tax ID numbers are used by the state to collect taxes. Check with your state department website to learn how to set up your tax ID number. If you have employees, you will likely need to send them a W-2 form at tax time. If you have a contracted employee or a vendor who has received more than $600 from you, you will need fill out a 1099 form for them for that tax year. I recommend that you work with an accountant or other tax professional like a CPA; they will tell you what forms you need to file and will also help you to take advantage of any deductions you may be eligible for.

BANKING - Set up a separate bank account for your business. Check rates and look into small business loans if this is something you might need, either now or in the future. Adopt a bookkeeping software or develop a system for managing your finances; stay organized from the beginning so you aren't pulling your hair out come tax season.

DBA

EIN

TAX ID

COPYRIGHT

Get ready for some big words: intellectual property is a category of intangible assets. Often, the core of your business is intangible: your brand name, designs, logo, and artwork.

Research copyright, trademarks, and patents to acquire a basic understanding and then find an intellectual property lawyer. Your business name is unique; I recommend that you register and trademark it.

COPYRIGHT YOUR WORK (OR NOT) - Maybe. It depends. Again, you should consult an attorney who specializes in intellectual property.

FAIR USE - In US copyright law, "Fair Use" allows brief excerpts of copyrighted material to be quoted for specific reasons and under specific circumstances.

That's so vague and CONFUSING. Am I right?! If you're a creative, get creative! Use your own original content and talk to a lawyer about protecting it. Again, don't take risks without consulting with a professional. You do not want to create an expensive problem that could have been easily avoided.

Believe it or not, large corporations knowingly steal from independent artists. Given this, it's a good idea to protect your work with copyright. If you're reading this, I hope you know that it's not okay to use someone's artwork without permission. Many small shops have had to remove their items because their artwork was using movie quotes or song lyrics that aren't in the public domain. It takes a long-ass time for something to become public domain, so make sure you do your research and get permission.

If you find someone stealing your work, I urge you not to let it slide. Sometimes a simple email will do the trick, but often you'll need to get a lawyer involved. Having your work already protected can be a defining factor when communicating with others who are using or misusing your work.

VISIT WWW.DMCA.COM TO LEARN ABOUT PROTECTING YOUR WEBSITE CONTENT.

POLICIES

If you're a shop owner, you won't have a "contract" with customers buying from your online shop. Instead, it's important to establish a set of policies. By purchasing from your shop, a customer agrees to your policies. If a "situation" arises, you can reference your policies as needed.

RETURN POLICY - How many days do customers have to return items? Can the items be opened? Are customers required to pay for return shipping? Do what works best for you and make sure your policies are very clearly communicated to your customers. Establish systems to easily implement your policy. For example, if you plan to supply return labels, make sure you know how to quickly and efficiently generate a label.

Let me warn you: at some point, you will undoubtedly receive an email from a customer who just cannot be satisfied. They may even threaten you with "horrible reviews" and that they will be "telling everyone"! It's up to you to decide when it's okay to break your policy to get someone off your back or when you feel it's important to stand firm. Think about what you would want the company to do for you, what is realistic, and how much you will lose or gain. I've found that when customers are polite, it's easy to offer them something for their troubles and they leave happier than ever. They tend to shout good reviews from the rooftops. On the other hand, when a customer is an a-hole, even if it's frustrating and difficult, finding a way to satisfy this person and get them off your back is probably worth quite a bit in the way of mental health. Ask yourself if the cost of keeping a client is less than the cost of losing them. If it's a simple situation that is clearly defined in your policies, remember that you put those terms in place for a reason and it's okay to refer back to them, even if someone isn't thrilled with the result.

SHIPPING - If you ship your products, make sure you live up to your policies. How many days do you take to ship items? How are they shipped? Priority? UPS®? USPS? Take this into account when you set up your policies and be sure you can deliver (no pun intended). It's a good idea to remind customers that once the item has left your facility (or spare bedroom), you cannot control what happens. If it gets lost in the mail, be prepared to file a claim. Have insurance on your packages. Know how to ship internationally and how long it will take for an item to arrive at a customer's location. Consider every scenario and make sure it's included in your policies. You will likely amend and revise your policy as you encounter new situations.

Craft your own shop policies informed by the research you've done. Make sure your policies are listed on your website and easily accessible by customers.

RETURN, EXCHANGE AND CANCELLATION POLICY

....

....

PAYMENT POLICY

....

....

SHIPPING SERVICE AND TIMES

....

....

ITEMS LOST IN THE MAIL

....

....

CUSTOM ORDERS

....

....

PRIVACY POLICY

....

....

LEGAL STUFF

NONDISCLOSURE FORMS - A nondisclosure form (aka an "NDA") is a confidentiality agreement. It's a document you sign committing to not share confidential information. Here's what it covers, in a nutshell: "Hey, let's work together. We're going to tell you secrets, but you can't share them. Here's what happens if you break the rules..." If a company shares an idea with you, they don't want you running off with it. You may ask customers to sign an NDA or a client may ask you to sign one. It's common, and you should be sure to read it over closely and understand it before signing. Can you share the images in your portfolio or on your social media? Are you allowed to acknowledge to others that you are working together?

CONTRACTS - Contracts and legal documents are intimidating, I get it. But they're also magical and life-saving. Rather than waiting until your foot is in your mouth and you can't pay this month's rent, get yourself a contract. From now until the end of time, you're using a contract.

A contract doesn't need to be long, scary, or confusing. But it does need to cover your ass. And your client's ass. There needs to be a lot of ass-covering all-around. You contract needs to be clear so that your clients understand what they're signing up for. A contract establishes you as a professional.

If a client sends *you* a contract, take your time to read it carefully and make sure you understand the document. If there is something you don't understand, ask for clarification. Try to imagine the worst-case scenario and ask yourself if the contract covers it. Think of a contract as the "who and what" for a project. It should state the scope of the project, fees, timeline, and important dates. It will also define the territory and usage, what changes are covered, reimbursable expenses, and a termination clause. Ownership of work should be clearly defined. Each time you book a new project, you will find more items to add or refine based on your accumulated experience. Hiring a lawyer to get you set up with a contract is a great idea, but there are also plenty of resources online. Start by drafting your own based on the information you find online and find a lawyer to review the draft once you feel good about it. Take your time and make sure your contract is worthy and understandable. An abbreviated sample contract is on the following page. All contracts or estimates should have an expiration date so you can't be held to old information.

YOUR
LOGO

Your name
Address
Email
Phone number

Client name
Address
Email
Phone number

PROJECT DESCRIPTION *Describe project, the details and who it is between.*

SCOPE *If the scope of the project increases, so does the fee. List what's included.*

ESTIMATE *The agreed upon price and payment plan that has been decided.*

PAYMENT *How payment will be delivered. 50% deposit due upon signing. The remainder of payment is due upon project completion. Client will be charged 1.5% per month until payment is received. Work will be halted if payment is not received.*

TIMELINE *Establish clear dates for each phrase of the project to hold yourself and your client accountable. Note what happens in case of delay.*

EXPLOITATION / COPYRIGHT *Make clear who owns the artwork. Does the client have exclusive rights? Ownership will not transfer until payment is made in full.*

MAINTENANCE *Is it a website that requires monthly maintenance? A mural that needs touch-ups?*

FILES *Are you sending digital or tangible files? Make sure you cover what happens with those files or tangible items.*

PROMOTION & CREDIT *How will this project be promoted? Is it being shared on both parties' social media accounts and websites? Does each party get credited?*

ADDITIONAL CHARGES *What might pop up as an additional fee; what isn't included in the scope.*

TERMINATION *If the client cancels the project halfway through, are they responsible for a kill fee? What is the penalty? How many days notice do you need? All outstanding work shall be paid for.*

By signing this contract you are agreeing to the terms above.

_____

Client Signature

_____

Date

_____

Your Signature

_____

Date

This contract is valid for 30 days. If unsigned, this contract expires on X date (or after 30 days)

CREATIVE BRIEFS & DELIVERABLES

CREATIVE BRIEFS - Creative briefs cover the scope of the project including the target market, competition, deliverables, and any other pertinent information. Think of it as a project overview.

PRESENTATION DECKS - A presentation deck is one of my favorite ways to impress a client. Demonstrate your value by creating a kick-ass presentation to introduce concepts and to give your client a glimpse into the quality of your work. Your presentation deck can include success stories, case studies, statistics, concepts, and pitches. Present your idea, educate about costs, and demonstrate the value you offer your client.

Since you're already over-delivering, a presentation deck is a no-brainer. In fact, any and all information you send to a client or customer should be on-brand and beautifully presented. A simple PDF in your brand voice is a great way to share pricing, pitches, policies, contracts, case studies, and other information.

For your presentation deck and any other client materials you require, create a template that you can customize for each client. This tells the client you'll bring your A-game when they work with you; it shows you're both professional and creative. Seize opportunities to infuse your brand, your voice, and your values into every part of your business, from your email signature to your invoices to your presentations. Each element is a way to remind your clients of your talent, professionalism, and another way to bring your creativity to the business side.

What information do you plan to include on your deliverables to educate and WOW your clients?

TAXES

Taxes can definitely be a headache. Put in the time up front to get and stay organized so that come tax time, you're prepared and ready to rock.

TAXES - Know that there are two types of taxes: income tax and sales tax. They're different.

SALES TAX - Sales tax is determined by your state and local governments. You are responsible for collecting sales tax on orders sold where you live. If you are in New York and you sell an item online in New York, you need to collect sales tax and deliver it to your state. Remitting your sales tax to your state may be required quarterly or annually depending on your volume of sales. You don't have to collect sales tax on wholesale orders; retailers are responsible for this. (Be sure to get a copy of their resale certificate.) Consult your state and local government websites to determine what you need to pay and when.

If you are earning income, you need to pay **income tax**. You pay taxes only where you operate. Check your local and state laws to make sure you have everything in check.

HIRING AN ACCOUNTANT - If you are profitable, I recommend that you hire an accountant or a CPA. A CPA is an accountant that has met additional requirements. Not all accountants are CPAs. For a few hundred dollars, they will help to make sure you have completed your taxes correctly and that you get any appropriate deductions. I use an online bookkeeping service that links to my credit cards and bank accounts. Once a month, I make sure that everything has been categorized correctly. I can easily look at up-to-date profit/loss information. The program allows me to easily create a Schedule C to hand to my CPA come tax time. I prefer to pay someone or purchase a program to take the stress out of doing my taxes so that I am free to focus on my creative work, but maybe you'd prefer doing it manually. Apparently some people enjoy math.

PUT MONEY ASIDE TO PAY YOUR TAXES - Regardless of whether you pay quarterly or annually, put money aside each month to pay for your taxes. It's easy to forget that it isn't already taken out and you don't want to be shocked when you owe thousands of dollars. It can be a hit to your bank account. Be prepared and make sure to note tax due dates on your calendar.

final thoughts

NOTES and TAKEAWAYS

That chapter was tough. Legal jargon can feel overwhelming, annoying, terrifying, and quite frankly, it sucks to sign a check giving your hard-earned money away. Get your ducks in a row from the beginning and you will save your future self from annoying headaches.

Now: you deserve a cookie.

CHAPTER 6

Goods & Services

Whether you create goods (cookies, stationery, custom signs, needlework) or provide services (photography, speech therapy, interior design) you are certainly keeping a lot of balls in the air at any one time. You may be trying to get your business off the ground and get your work in front of clients or you may be overwhelmed by the volume of work you have and thinking about scaling up. This chapter speaks to some common circumstances and scenarios faced by creative small business owners, from advice on how to navigate tricky conversations (such as requests to work for exposure) to how to approach daunting tasks (such as how to find a reputable manufacturer).

THE GOODS

If you own or want to own a product shop, the following few pages are for you! I have always had products to sell. In high school, I crocheted hats and sold them to my friends and family. I briefly sold makeup to raise money for my swim team. No surprise given my love of typography, I started a stationery line in 2011. I started by selling on Etsy and at local craft shows before later moving onto wholesale (more on this later).

It's important to consider how many products you want to offer initially. Think through the logistics of creating, storing, selling, and distributing your goods:

HOW MANY PRODUCTS DO YOU PLAN TO SELL INITIALLY?

WHAT ARE THE COSTS (TIME AND MONEY) ASSOCIATED WITH PRODUCING THESE PRODUCTS?

CAN YOU AFFORD TO WORK WITH A MANUFACTURER OR CAN YOU MAKE YOUR PRODUCTS YOURSELF?

IF YOU OPT TO HAVE YOUR PRODUCTS MANUFACTURED, CAN YOU GET A PROTOTYPE? IS THERE A MINIMUM? CAN YOU TAKE PRE-ORDERS?

WHERE WILL YOU STORE YOUR PRODUCTS? DO YOU NEED TO RENT OFFICE OR STORAGE SPACE, OR DO YOU HAVE A SPARE BEDROOM OR GARAGE YOU CAN UTILIZE?

WILL PEOPLE BUY YOUR PRODUCTS ONLINE, IN STORES, OR BOTH?

HOW WILL YOU DISTRIBUTE YOUR PRODUCTS?

MANUFACTURING

There are two primary reasons to consider working with a manufacturer: either you are making a product you can't produce on your own (perhaps your product requires heavy or expensive machinery) or you need to quickly and efficiently produce your product in large quantities. If or when you decide to work with a manufacturer, be prepared for the process to involve a lot of trial and error. You'll need to give yourself plenty of lead time to do research (read reviews, interview the manufacturer's current clients, get prototypes, etc.). The process can be even more difficult if you're creating something that has never before been produced. Know that a perfect partnership won't form overnight.

When you are just starting out, it is almost always the most economical to make your products yourself if at all possible. Print at home, buy paper in bulk, fold each card, ship each order. When you're ready to scale up, look into manufacturing. Know that you will be required to order in large quantities. Of course, the hit you take in price will be what you gain in time to focus on other important things.

Printed items can be produced domestically or overseas. Consider price, reliability, shipping, and lead times before you decide where to manufacture your products.

When you are ready to research manufacturers, here are some questions to consider: Do you already know anyone who manufactures? Who can you "interview"? What are the set-up charges? What's the estimated turnaround time? What is the minimum production run? What are the price breaks? Does the manufacturer have the ability to produce/print on-demand? Can the manufacturer store/warehouse products? What are the payment terms?

Most companies offer a line of products, however, some offer one unique, high-end product with a few variations (color or pattern, for example). Research your industry to learn what works best and how this compares to what you currently produce.

WHOLESALE 101

Here are some of the important logistical concerns if you plan to wholesale:

NUMBER OF PRODUCTS - How many products will you offer? Can you offer a variety of colors or styles of the same product?

PRICING - In the wholesale world, the formula typically looks like this:

COST OF GOODS* X 2 = WHOLESALE COST

WHOLESALE X 2 = RETAIL COST

Whatever your product, don't forget to factor in YOUR payment, YOUR time, packaging, printing, and any other associated costs. Research your industry to make sure your product pricing falls within an acceptable range.

WHOLESALE CALENDAR - Get ready for Christmas in January! Boutiques order for holidays and special seasons far in advance. Develop a calendar to help you track retailer schedules and deadlines. Ask companies when they typically order for Valentine's Day or Halloween and work backward from that date to give yourself ample lead time to create, produce, promote, and ship your products.

INVENTORY - Bust out those spreadsheets! It is crucial to keep careful track of inventory to be prepared for orders, restocking, and to avoid last-minute scrambles. Keep your list up-to-date or use an online service that links to your shop to help you to ship and track your inventory.

CATALOG - Before you're ready to reach out to customers (via email or in-person), you should prepare a beautifully designed catalog complete with a list of your products, accompanying photographs, pricing, SKU numbers, and policies. Make it easy for people to order! You can also set up a wholesale portal on your website.

COLLECTING PAYMENT - "Net 30" means that the purchaser is expected to pay within 30 days of receiving goods. Do you require payment before shipping? What works best for you? (Would Target® ship to you before you paid? Nope.) If you have a strong relationship with a regular, trustworthy client, you may consider a signed agreement allowing them to pay quarterly.

The fun part of wholesale, of course, is finding retail homes for your amazing products! There are a number of ways to go about finding shops to carry your work:

STORES - Start local! There are likely many beautiful shops right in your own town. Walk around trendy retail neighborhoods; bring samples and hand out and collect business card. Face-to-face is a great way to introduce yourself! Be sure your elevator speech is ready to go. Window shop on vacation and seize the opportunity to scout new shops. Know that smaller boutiques and shops may want to sell your work on consignment, meaning they will take your inventory and pay you once they sell it. Often, your commission will be larger than it is with wholesale (60/40), but each store is different.

ONLINE - You can also rely on social media and old-fashioned Internet searches to uncover new businesses to reach out to. Get comfortable emailing stores that could potentially carry your products. Do your research and make a point to explain WHY their customers will love your products. Don't be frustrated if you don't hear anything in return. This is often the nature of cold-calling. However, definitely make a point to check back in when you have a new product or special promotion. Sometimes timing is everything.

DROP SHIP/ PRINT ON DEMAND - There are some great drop ship and print-on-demand sites. You simply upload your work and you can have it printed on just about anything! This option allows you to offer a range of products, or to simply test a product before you produce it yourself. On the downside, margins are low and these sites tend to be inundated with designs. It can be challenging to make your products stand out and may be too costly for wholesale.

SALES REPS - Your line is doing great and you want to continue to grow, but you can't keep up with it yourself. This is a good problem to have! At this point, you may want to consider working with a sales rep. Find one who works with your style of work and reach out for a conversation. You can also set up an affiliate program with your repeat customers or create a brand ambassador program.

Selling wholesale is a great way to get your products in more hands. And there's no doubt about it, it can be thrilling to see your product featured in a cute, brick-and-mortar shop or your favorite online shop. While there are benefits to selling wholesale, there are also some important things to be aware of. Working with retailers—especially big retailers—is a whole other level of logistical planning. The turn-around time can be tight and the profit margins low. It's absolutely okay to only sell directly to your customers and to altogether eschew wholesale.

Once you have established a few successful store relationships, consider exhibiting at a trade show. These shows are typically a lot of work, but many shop owners attend in search of new products to buy.

BLOGGERS

Bloggers are influencers. Companies approach bloggers and send free products in exchange for a sponsored post about the product. Bloggers appeal to large companies because their influence feels more human, as opposed to a "corporate" feel that lacks a personal touch. Followers may feel like they know a blogger from watching her Instagram stories or from reading and commenting on blog posts or conversations on Twitter.

The best bloggers are authentic and share only products they love. Don't blindly send your product and expect that the blogger will automatically post about it. It's best to try to establish some sort of connection or relationship; take the time to engage with the blogger/influencer through social media. Any item you do send should fit their brand and be something that will genuinely appeal to them. Discuss the specifics of the collaboration before you send something.

The same rules of thumb apply to sponsorships. Work only with sponsors who align with your values and are a good fit for your audience. Don't work with someone just because they're willing to pay you.

Write down three bloggers you think would be a great fit for your brand.

1. ....

2. ....

3. ....

STYLED SHOOTS

I have contributed paper goods to many styled shoots and have very rarely been paid. I've traded product because what I received was equal in value; I appreciated the opportunity to have beautiful photos of my work. A styled shoot is usually done for a feature on a major site (or for fun!) and has the potential to put your work in front of dream clients and lead to great jobs. However, depending on your craft, you may be asked to contribute more than you are comfortable with. I recommend that you first have a conversation with the organizers so you fully understand what is being asked of you. Be honest about the time and resources you can devote to the shoot. In my experience, these conversations are usually productive and it's exciting to find ways to work together.

I THINK THE *moment* THAT I THINK I'VE MADE IT IS THE *moment I* SHOULD *no* LONGER BE IN *this* JOB

MALLORY BLAIR

CEO AT SMALL GIRLS PR | SMALLGIRLSPR.COM | @YOURPALMAL

SERVICES

If you work as a consultant, do design work, or offer anything else that isn't held in your hand (writing, photography, etc.), you are a service provider. Of course, a service and a product can often go hand-in-hand, like when a photographer takes the photos *and* offers prints for sale.

When you start out, you may be hungry for every opportunity. You want experience and you may be willing to charge less to make sure you get the job. I get it. However, you need to value yourself and your expertise. Begin with an estimate of how many hours the job will take and multiply that by your hourly rate. This is your base fee. Next, add a buffer: some projects will go over and some will stay under. Account for supplies you'll need and factor this cost into your rate. Also consider that you will need to put money back into your business, into your retirement account, and set some aside for taxes. In other words, the entire payment you receive will not go directly into your pocket. Consider all factors and adjust your fees accordingly.

Remember our pricing discussion from the last chapter? You will likely need to offer different fee structures for different situations. If a client approaches you directly for a project you do often and specialize in (photographing a wedding, a branding package, etc), a flat fee might be best. If you are hired by an agency to freelance for a day, you will likely be paid by the hour. Know that if you do charge by the hour, clients often don't have an accurate grasp on how many hours a project will take. If you're a painter, muralist, or work with installations, you may charge by the square foot. A flat fee can help you to avoid undercharging once you get a grasp on your process, and the client. However, recall that it can be useful to offer tiered pricing options to demonstrate your value. Also know that if you start high, a client can (and will!) try to negotiate down. If you start low, it's almost impossible to ask for more.

Scope creep is when a client is asking for something that's outside of the project scope. Not to worry, just kindly explain to them that you're happy to do that, at your hourly rate of $X. Include this in your contract so they're aware they can scale up as needed and it won't come as a surprise. Consider if the project will prohibit you from taking on others. Make sure your contract reflects what is (and isn't!) included in the job. Are there three revisions? One in-person meeting? Write that sh*t down.

The beauty of being a small business owner is that you get to establish your own value. Charge fairly and appropriately for each client and project, while educating your clients about your industry and your unique talent.

FREELANCE AIN'T FREE

You're talented and you should be paid for your services. It's that simple. Your time has value. Your talent has value. That said, there are still people out there who may not fully appreciate what you're doing. It's okay to say no to someone who asks you to work for free. You can offer a canned response such as this: "As a small business owner, I'm sure you can understand that I can't work without being compensated." Or simply decline because you're busy (with paying clients). If you decide to work for free, you should feel like you're getting something out of it, be it a good feeling, the creative freedom to try something new, or the opportunity to get your work in front of people who you really want to see it

Let's talk about some situations you may (ahem, almost certainly) find yourself in:

WORKING WITH FRIENDS & FAMILY - Proceed with caution; there is definitely potential for things to get uncomfortable. If you do choose to work with friends or family, the most important thing is to keep it professional. Treat them the way you'd treat a client! WRITE A CONTRACT. Say no if you don't think things will go smoothly. Make sure they've seen your work and want to work with you because of your style, not just because you're capable. However, if you do get an opportunity to work with a friend or family member, don't forget that they will be your greatest form of free advertising. Impress them and they'll tell everyone about their talented friend/relative who they should hire. (Thanks, Mom!)

TRADES - Think about whether the trade feels equal in value. "Value" can mean hours or monetary value, but it should feel beneficial for both parties. Don't trade just because someone's offering. If you do decide to trade, create a contract so everyone is on the same page.

PRO-BONO - When you're starting out (and anytime, really) doing pro-bono work for non-profit organizations (or another meaningful organization) is a wonderful way to boost your portfolio (and your ego). Some organizations may even be able to cover the cost of supplies. You may (and should) be given the creative freedom to dream up a really great project for an organization and cause you care about.

WORKING FOR EXPOSURE (OR NOT)

This is a topic I feel strongly about. Companies (both large and small) may ask you to do or provide something in exchange for "exposure." This is really prevalent, especially in the social media age. It often amounts to someone asking you to create something for their company without actually paying you to do so. They want to support you—without actually supporting you. Typically, "exposure" is a feature on the company's website or social media account with an attribution—but without any further guarantees.

Here's an example from my dad. (Hi, Dad!) A bottling company donates bottled water for an event. Here, they're literally able to put their product into consumer's hands. There is a high chance they will convert customers. It's an opportunity for marketing. There is a clear benefit to the bottling company. However, small businesses face a different challenge when working for exposure. It's less certain they will recoup time, money, and resources. Do you see the difference?

Ask yourself these questions before you commit to work for exposure:

- **WILL THIS BRING ME ANY SORT OF FULFILLMENT?**
- **WHAT WOULD I CHARGE SOMEONE FOR THIS?**
- **WHY IS IT OKAY FOR ME TO DO IT FOR FREE IN THIS INSTANCE?**
- **WILL THIS STRENGTHEN MY PORTFOLIO? HOW?**
- **WHAT IS THE EXPOSURE? WHO IS THE AUDIENCE?**
- **IS THERE POTENTIAL TO ATTRACT NEW WORK/CLIENTS THROUGH THIS EXPOSURE?**

Tread very carefully if you consider working for exposure. Exposure doesn't pay the rent. (Dolla dolla bills, ya'll!) It is not a guarantee of anything. Exposure doesn't appropriately value your work or talent. It is seldom a mutually beneficial arrangement.

FREELANCE ain't FREE

GO TIME

If you are launching a new line, collection, product, service, or business, you want to plan ahead and work hard to build up excitement. Celebrate every little thing! Work backward to create an action plan for your next launch. Think of every task you'll need to do to prepare, from designing products and approving proofs to marketing materials and email campaigns.

6 - 9 MONTHS OUT

3 - 6 MONTHS OUT

1 - 3 MONTHS OUT

At three months out, look for places to share your story. Hype your launch day on social media to get people excited and interested. Set up a mailing list for people to get the news delivered to their sacred inbox.

2 - 4 WEEKS OUT

Write a press release! Send it to relevant blogs, media outlets, and influencers.

LAUNCH DAY

Cue the confetti!!!! Send an email, share on social, ask your friends to share, and TELL EVERYONE! Then PARTY! You made something amazing; be proud of yourself!

YOU
DON'T HAVE
TO GET IT

Perfect

YOU JUST
HAVE TO GET
IT

going

MARIE FORLEO

final thoughts

NOTES and TAKEAWAYS

You crushed another chapter! You should be proud! You're taking all the right steps to make your brand even bigger than you are. You're sharing it with the world and the world is excited to hear about it, buy it, and admire it!

CHAPTER 7

Making the Wheels Turn

Let me tell you a secret: there are never enough hours in the day. Who decided twenty-four hours was sufficient? I'd like to have a word with them.

If you're a small business owner, your to-do list is never-ending. But it can be tamed. The following chapter is all about how to work smart, maximize your productivity, delegate, and set realistic expectations. You'll think about what you want your work life to look like and what you want your personal life to look like, and whether this is achievable. (Spoiler: it is!) Remember: YOU are the boss. You are carrying a lot of responsibility, but you also have the power to build the life—professional and personal—that you want!

WORK ENVIRONMENT

Some people can't understand how I've worked from my home office for over three years; others totally get it. It's important to find out how and where you work the best. While I love that I don't *have* to wear pants at home, I also know that I'm at my best and my most productive when I get up, get dressed, and tackle my day with enthusiasm (and pants).

Are you too easily distracted to work at home? Will the mess in the kitchen or the goodies in the pantry keep you from getting your tasks done? Will working at home mean you never leave the house again? Find what is best for your working style. It might be getting up early and going to your favorite coffee shop, a co-working space, a dedicated home office space, or another arrangement.

Even though I (currently) love working from home and I'm able to do so effectively, I have also found that weekly visits to the library, coffee shop, or co-working space revitalizes me. I love the change of pace, the fresh air, the white noise, and the chance to absorb the positive energy of people around me. Also, fancy drinks are delicious. An office space is an additional expense, so consider your budget and see if it makes sense. I've found that it's helpful to designate a space in my home for my office. It's helpful for me to create that separation, even if I do still bring my computer to the couch on occasion.

I genuinely miss having colleagues, so I've made it a point to stay in touch with other work-from-home designers. I even have a bi-weekly Mastermind where we video chat and talk about the ups and downs of our business.

If you've got a lot of other responsibilities, it can feel hard (nah, impossible!) to get a second to yourself. But, it's amazing how productive you can be with a block of distraction-free time. Find one block of time each week where you can be alone and focused and use that time to hustle! You'll turn into an octopus during this time, crushing eight items off your to-do list at once. You're incredible!

HOME OFFICE

PRO	CON
No pants!	Talking to the dog too much

STUDIO SPACE

PRO	CON
People to talk to	Pants

HIRING HELP

First, you're not a freshly baked cookie. You can't be everything to everyone, and you don't want to be! Stop humble bragging about how busy you are and hire help. I don't care if help comes in the form of a robot, an app, or a real-life human, it's okay to ask for help.

Wouldn't it be nice if your business could run without you? For a lot of us, that doesn't seem like it will ever be the case. We *are* our business. However, you can still find places to hire help. It's a big step and there are a lot of things to consider. It's easy to feel like you won't find someone that can think and create exactly as you do, but luckily, you can teach someone the ropes. Ask for referrals and test someone with a project before you hire them full-time. Remember that it takes time to train someone properly, but in the long run, you will be free to focus on what you do best.

There are many ways to find employees. For example, post in a Facebook group—there may just be a young, malleable candidate who wants to learn the ropes. Check local universities for interns. Perhaps you're willing to work with someone remotely, but you can ask around locally, too.

Whomever you hire, make sure to set up an employment agreement. Make your expectations clear, even if they seem obvious, and include them in the agreement so everyone is on the same page.

CONTRACTED EMPLOYEES - Consider if you can use someone on a per project basis or if you need someone full-time.

OFFERING BENEFITS - If you hire someone on a freelance basis, you won't offer benefits. However, if you plan to hire someone full-time now or in the future, benefits are something to think about.

RETAINER TEAM - Another option is to have help on retainer. This means that you pay someone a set dollar amount per month (or per pay period) and send your needs during that time frame. Set boundaries to make sure the relationship is beneficial for everyone.

DO WHAT YOU DO **BEST**, *hire* OUT THE **REST**

—MILES ZATKOWSKY (DAD)

LIMITS

Even if you hire help, your own to-do list will feel endless. There will always be more ways to promote your work, more projects to tackle, more client to seek. Recognize your limits, establish smart boundaries, and stick to them as much as you can. Take care of yourself and try to achieve some sort of balance in your life.

Some people prefer to "block" their time, scheduling meetings or administrative work on certain days of the week. For example, I have set a recurring monthly event on my calendar to review accounting. Set your ideal working hours and try to stick to them. These are just a few ways to stay on top of your game and be productive.

HOW MANY PROJECTS CAN YOU MANAGE PER MONTH?

HOW MANY PROJECTS CAN YOU TAKE ON PER WEEK?

HOW MANY DAYS PER WEEK CAN YOU WORK?

HOW MANY HOURS CAN YOU WORK?

WHAT HOURS DO YOU WORK BEST?

WHICH HOURS ARE THOSE?

WHEN DO YOU NEED TO UNPLUG?

HOW MANY MEETINGS CAN YOU MANAGE PER WEEK?

WHICH DAYS DO YOU PREFER FOR MEETINGS?

DELEGATING

DON'T WANT TO DO	CAN'T DO IT ALL	NOT COMPETENT

TIME MANAGEMENT & PRODUCTIVITY

I was born with the productivity gene. Organizational tools excite me. I even designed a planner that kick-started my own journey as a business owner. I love to-do lists and deadlines. I truly live by the phrase "On time is late, early is on time."

I manage to-do lists by breaking them into time frames that will allow me to accomplish everything I need to. I keep daily, weekly, and monthly to do-lists; this helps me to focus on the big picture, as well as the small tasks along the way. I write a new daily list at the end of each day so that I already know what I need to do when I get to my desk the next morning.

Be realistic about what you can accomplish in a day. Define no more than three high-priority tasks that you are confident you can complete. You will be more likely to stay on track, setting yourself up for success! To maximize your productivity, break those tasks into smaller, actionable items. For example, "publish four blog posts" might include "write blog posts" and "create graphics." Identifying smaller steps allows you to cross things off your list—and dang, that feels good!

You can also increase your efficiency by "blocking" parts of the day for dedicated tasks. Create blocks of focused time for one task, take a break, and then move to another task. Shorts breaks allow you to refocus. You'll train your productivity just like a muscle. There are several specific, published methodologies out there that you can look to for advice. My go-to here is The Pomodoro Technique®. You'll be amazed at how much you can accomplish in a brief but focused block of time.

BILLING

The Internet makes it so easy to set up invoices and payment plans and to accept credit cards. If you set up a business bank account, you can use an online billing service. You can send contracts, request signatures, and send invoices. There are plenty of options to choose from, including Freshbooks®, Square™ and Dubsado. Be sure to compare what each service has to offer and the associated cost. Make sure you're getting paid in a professional way and be wary of apps that are built for sending money to friends.

THE POMODORO TECHNIQUE: DO MORE AND HAVE FUN
WITH TIME MANAGEMENT BY FRANCESCO CIRILLO

On time **IS** LATE,
EARLY **IS** On time

BATCHING

Do you know someone who seems to effortlessly manage to "do it all"? Let me tell you a secret: they DON'T! First, stop comparing yourself to others. People have different sets of priorities and different thresholds for stress and work.

It's important to look at your workload with an objective eye. Which items on your to-do list bring you joy? Which items can be delegated to someone else?

There are tons of systems designed to help your business run smoothly: invoicing, bookkeeping, and even social media scheduling. For small business owners, the mountains of "little things" you need to attend to each week can feel overwhelming. "Batching" can be a great strategy. For example, set aside an hour each week or an entire day each month to do all of your social media scheduling. If you run a product shop, maybe you only ship on Tuesdays and Thursdays (just be sure to state your shipping times on your website & policies). Batching helps you to stay organized and not feel overly burdened by the tasks at hand.

What activities can you batch, and when?

INBOX ZEROish

Do you fantasize about having zero email and nothing to do but put your feet up and relax? Have you ever experienced such joy? Probably not! In today's world, emails land in your inbox with lightning speed and it's hard to keep up. Instead of making your goal "inbox zero," let's talk about how to tame your inbox.

It's important to use a user-friendly email platform that allows you to quickly and easily organize your email communication. I use Gmail™. It's free, user-friendly, and I can easily manage the emails I receive. The most professional option is to use an address with your domain name (name@yourwebsite.com). You can set this up to forward to any email platform.

Not everyone works this way, but my inbox functions as my to-do list. An email that sits in my inbox is one that requires action. Once I have taken that action and am awaiting a reply, I will manually "archive" the email into a folder I have designated for that particular project so that I can reference it later as needed. If additional follow-up is required, I note it in my calendar and set a notification for a few days later.

When it comes to promotions, I "unsubscribe" as often as possible. Trust me: you don't need the email (and mental) clutter.

> CANNED EMAIL RESPONSES ARE A SMART WAY TO SAVE TIME. WHENEVER YOU SEND A SOMEWHAT "GENERIC" EMAIL, SAVE IT AS A CANNED RESPONSE. WRITE A CANNED RESPONSE FOR INQUIRY EMAILS, QUESTIONS ABOUT RETURNS, SHIPPING DETAILS, ETC.

Gmail Labs™ are add-ons to supercharge your email. Take a look at all the options they have so you can customize your inbox.

Mailboost and Boomerang® are awesome plug-ins for Gmail that allow you to schedule your emails to send later. Your clients don't need to know if you're working at 2am.

Newton™ is an email app that connects all your accounts. It schedules emails and has a "read receipts" function that tells you if someone has read your email.

Polymail® is a similar app that allows you to stay connected, organized, and on top of your sh*t.

TIME MANAGEMENT	ROUTINE

TIME MANAGEMENT

I get it, time management doesn't come naturally to everyone. Netflix® is calling your name, as well as a ton of other obligations, chores, and tasks. When you work for yourself, you need to stay on top of your tasks. Break them up, and set yourself up for success.

ROUTINE

MORNING ROUTINE -

NIGHT TIME ROUTINE -

DAILY	DAILY

DAILY

-
-
-
-
-
-
-

DAILY

-
-
-
-
-
-
-

WEEKLY

-
-
-
-
-
-
-
-

WEEKLY

-
-
-
-
-
-
-

MONTHLY

- BOOKKEEPING - *Make sure every thing is accounted for and up to date.*

- NEWSLETTER - *New launch? Sales? Send an update!*

- BATCH - *Mark your calendar for your batch days: social media or painting days. Write it down!*

-
-
-

MONTHLY

BEING PROFESSIONAL

One of my favorite "tricks" is to under-promise and over-deliver. This means you're going to blow your client's mind. You'll gain respect by acting professionally at all times. Your personality can shine through (of course!) but you take your job seriously and consistently bring your passion and creativity to the table. You insist on a contract and have your ducks in a row. When you tell your client you will have files to them by Friday morning, you send the files by EOD Thursday. When you have a 9am meeting, you arrive at 8:50 with a hot coffee for your client in hand.

How can you convey professionalism and impress your clients?

THROW PERFECTION OUT THE WINDOW

Attention to detail is necessary and you definitely want to provide quality and value. Cutting corners can lead to poor quality, but also consider that perfectionism can waste a ton of time! Figure out where it's useful to insist on being perfect and where you can ease up a little. So much of a creative business is behind the scenes when no one is watching, and it's fine to get a little messy. It's also human to mess up, and it's okay to tell your clients that you've done so.

Are there areas in which you can let go a bit and release yourself from the expectation to be perfect?

Under
PROMISE
OVER DELIVER
every single
TIME

JENNA KUTCHER

INSPIRATION

I often wonder where my next idea will come from. Sometimes I lose sleep over this. Usually, I need to take a few deep breaths and allow myself to just be. When I can do this, I find that inspiration strikes in unexpected ways: from time spent outdoors, trying a new food, or a new workout. Ideas will come. You can't force them, but you can experience the world with a creative spirit. The more you enjoy life, the more inspired you'll feel! Working more isn't going to generate a magical idea. Give yourself time. Make a list of ways you get inspired:

....

....

....

....

....

HUSTLE

Hustle looks different to everyone. I'm not sure why we collectively glorify living our lives at top speed. I'm here to remind you that while it's important to work hard, it's also important to live your life. When we are our best selves, our businesses will naturally shine.

You've heard the phrase "Fake it until you make it." Is there truth to this? Well, yes and no. I find that it's good to be human and honest. Talk about your business with confidence, but also be willing to admit where you struggle. Have you received an inquiry that's too good to pass up, but it's something you've haven't done before? Tell the client you're confident you can make magic, and what you'll need to get it done. Then dive in and learn everything you can to make it happen.

If you're a personal brand, sharing your real life struggles makes you appear more human. People are into YOU and they're following your unique story. I challenge you to get real and even a little vulnerable. I'll bet that you find a lot of people who can relate.

RAPID FIRE

If you feel stuck, sometimes a rapid fire idea session is helpful. Use this page to write down anything that comes to mind when you're trying to come up with an idea or solution. NOTHING is too dumb to write down; you never know what it could spark! Set a timer for 20 minutes and brainstorm!

WORD CLOUD - Another way to get past a creative block is to try a good old-fashioned word cloud! Write down everything that comes to mind, and don't toss out any ideas as "bad." I'll bet you surprise yourself with what you can come up with!

START HERE

MENTAL HEATH & BURNOUT

You might ask yourself "Will I ever get to take a vacation?" I get it, and the answer is YES! You're the boss, remember? You make the schedule! Stop thinking that running around without a moment to breathe is what makes you successful. Set yourself up to work smarter, not harder!

Do your clients expect you to be at their beck and call? Why? I recommend that you establish realistic and reasonable expectations at the beginning. Schedule more time than you think you need for each project to allow yourself a comfortable amount of time for completion and to accommodate unforeseen issues that may arise.

It's hard to be your own boss. You have to hold yourself accountable for shutting off that computer at a reasonable hour. It's important to follow through on your commitments, and equally important to take care of yourself.

Consider ways you can gracefully communicate your boundaries. How about listing your working hours in your email signature? Schedule your emails to be sent during normal working hours so that you don't unwittingly give someone the impression that you work into the wee hours (even if you occasionally do!).

Work/life balance can feel elusive, but you can strive to build your work and personal life into something that feels right for you.

Make a list of "self-care" practices: a yoga class, a pedicure, a daily walk, time with friends, or a glass of wine in the evening. What rejuvenates you?

BALANCE

Balance. There's that word again. People talk about "work/life balance," but does such a thing really exist? I'm honestly not sure!

I know that when you're passionate about your work, it's always on your mind to some degree. It's important to find ways to take a break, to recharge, and to spend time with people who love and support you. Take time to think about what "balance" means to you. Also acknowledge that "balance" is a moving target. One day you might pull a long day (or night!) at the office; you might devote another day to family time or self-care.

"Balance" comes in many forms. Perhaps it's shutting off your computer at 5:00, or working late once a week. Perhaps it's ladies night once a month or yoga twice a week. Give thought to what your priorities are and what makes you your best self. Make time for what is important to you, even when you feel like you don't have the time. You won't regret it.

What does balance look like for you?

IDEAL DAYS

Self-care is a bit of a buzz word, but I believe that it's really important—especially for entrepreneurs. There was a time when I felt like all I did was work and that I was missing out on everything. Think about it: if you work really long days or if you continue to work after-hours, it's tempting to grab fast food, skip the work out, and skimp on sleep. This is a recipe for a crash-and-burn—and you don't want that! Using a schedule helped me to carve out time for myself and I felt like I got my life back. Take the time to think about what your "ideal day" looks like, knowing that it'll adjust with demands of work and personal life. Consider when you feel the most productive or the most creative. Are you a night owl or a morning person? Be sure to schedule time for yourself: take a walk, sit down for a real meal, read a book. And at the risk of sounding like your mother, make sure you drink plenty of water and get plenty of sleep!

5 am		3 pm	
6 am		4 pm	
7 am		5 pm	
8 am		6 pm	
9 am		7 pm	
10 am		8 pm	
11 am		9 pm	
12 pm		10 pm	
1 pm		11 pm	
2 pm			

M

T

W

TH

F

SAT

SUN

final thoughts

NOTES and TAKEAWAYS

Another chapter bites the dust! You're delegating, taking care of yourself, and batching your work like the BOSS you are! You're surprising, delighting, and crushing it with your clients—they notice. Those inquiries are coming in hot and you're basically a professional juggler now. I'm impressed.

CHAPTER 8

Evaluation and Reflection

If you have made it this far, you have experienced some pivotal moments. I know you've had moments of doubt—probably lots of them. I would bet my piggy bank that you have surprised yourself, too—that you have done things that you never dreamed you could do. And through it all, I know that you have learned a lot about yourself.

Learning and growing is an ongoing process. You may never feel like you "have it all together," but it's so important to acknowledge all you have learned and just how far you have come.

In this chapter, you'll reflect on work you have done and all you have learned. And you'll think about how to use what you've learned to continue to set new goals to chase after. Work hard. Dream big. Learn and grow. That's what it's all about. I'm so proud of you.

Record notes about projects you have worked on or clients you have worked with. Do you notice any patterns emerge?

CLIENT	HOW THEY FOUND YOU	PROJECT	BUDGET

TIMELINE	NOTES

JOURNALING

It's important to reflect. Take time to celebrate what you've done well. Consider what has worked for you and what has not.

WHAT AM I BEST AT?

WHAT HAS SURPRISED ME?

WHAT CAN I DO BETTER?

WHAT HAVE I LEARNED?

WHAT DO I WANT TO LEARN?

WHAT HAS PROVEN TO BE SUCCESSFUL?

WHAT ARE MY FAVORITE WAYS TO RELIEVE STRESS?

KEEP TRUCKIN'

Failure is inevitable. It's okay: look at failure as an opportunity to learn and grow. For every "YES" you hear, you will probably hear "NO" far more frequently. That's just reality. There will be a lot of emails left unread, clients you don't book, or abandoned checkouts in your online shop. Don't take it personally. Take a look at what's working and what's not, and think about how you can adjust and pivot to improve.

WHAT WORKED	WHAT DIDN'T

TALLY OF TIMES YOU'VE FALLEN, BUT GOTTEN BACK UP:

ENOUGH

IS A

decision

NOT AN

amount

ALISON FAULKNER

WRITER, SPEAKER, DANCER | THEALISONSHOW.COM | @THEALISONSHOW

KIND WORDS

Write down testimonials from your clients and come back to them when you need a pick me up!

PASSIVE INCOME

Passive Income sounds AMAZING right?! Kick back, watch TV with a pint of ice cream and a beverage in hand, and watch those dollars roll in! Not quite the case when it comes to passive income. Passive income takes a lot of upfront work and a ton of consistent marketing to stay in the front of peoples' minds. Think about it: anyone can start a shop, so it's that much more difficult to stand out online. You need to put in the time to create unique, memorable pieces, and you also have to devote time to promote your product like crazy, not to mention the time you'll spend on maintenance and customer service.

Some ideas for "passive income" include printable wall art, worksheets, patterns, templates, and courses. Courses are a lot of work but they command a higher price point and allow you to share your knowledge and experience with others. A popular Instagram post can turn into a podcast episode; a blog post can turn into an audiobook. Think about how you can repurpose (and enhance) your content. Make it accessible to more people by offering similar content in different mediums. Brainstorm "passive income" ideas and remember to think about how to position these ideas for potential customers.

REVIEWS

In addition to testimonials, you have probably also gotten some great feedback. If you haven't, be sure to ask for it! In fact, you should consider asking for feedback a standard step in your process. Create a survey that asks your customers for ways you can improve. Have a tough skin: be willing to accept constructive criticism, but also take feedback with a grain of salt. If you own a product shop, you can respond quickly to any negative reviews that can be resolved (not hateful comments). Demonstrate that you are a professional. You have the opportunity to turn someone's negative experience around.

Write down any areas in which your clients or customers have expressed dissatisfaction and brainstorm ways in which you might improve. Don't worry, the praise comes on the next page!

HUMBLE BRAG

It may feel uncomfortable, but you have to be able to speak confidently about your talent and skills. Use this page to write down some of your shining moments and praise you've received from your clients. Celebrate even small victories! Remember: if you're not able to talk about your work with enthusiasm and pride, how will someone be confident in hiring you?

BUG LIST

It's important to note the things that bug you—the behaviors and circumstances that make your skin crawl and create sleepless nights. Is it a client who works best at night (when you're asleep and hear your phone buzzing in your dreams)? Is it someone who writes multiple emails throughout the day, or can't seem to wait 24 hours for a response? Is it anything involving spreadsheets? As you work with more clients and gain experience, keep a list of the things that "bug" you or that don't allow you to create your best work. Refer back to this list as you consider new clients to make sure they are right for you. Consider these as red flags when they pop up.

Make sure your contracts help to prevent circumstances where you feel taken advantage of and do everything you can to educate your clients about the value of your work. You don't want to find yourself in small claims court trying to justify that your hours of research and discovery for their project is worth payment. It's hard to put a price tag on the creative process and it can be difficult to explain what you do to people outside of your field. We are experts in our fields and should be treated accordingly. Not everyone understands this, and it's important that you listen to your gut if you don't think a client is going to be the right fit for you.

Use the page on the right to note things that bother you: late payments, people who expect you to be on call 24/7, and so on. Remember that if it's going to be difficult, and unenjoyable on your end, it's probably won't be a fun experience for the client, either.

When you realize a client isn't the right fit for you, consider if they might be perfect for someone else. Reach for your list of industry friends, and refer them to someone you think will do a great job with the project. They'll return the favor one day, and supporting each other makes the world go round.

BUG LIST

- ....
- ....
- ....
- ....
- ....
- ....
- ....
- ....
- ....
- ....
- ....
- ....
- ....
- ....
- ....
- ....
- ....
- ....

IN A PICKLE

You will inevitably run into difficult situations. It can be tough to maintain proper perspective, but it's critical to do so. Here are some tough-love questions you can ask yourself when you're in a pickle.

- **SHOULD I WORK WITH A CLIENT I DON'T AGREE WITH?**
- **CAN I USE THE MONEY FROM "BAD" JOB TO INSPIRE "GOOD"?**
- **WHAT IS THE DURATION OF THE PROJECT?**
- **WILL THIS INTERFERE WITH MY VALUES?**
- **WHERE DO I DRAW THE LINE?**
- **WILL THIS PROJECT BENEFIT ME OR OTHERS?**

SWEET SPOT

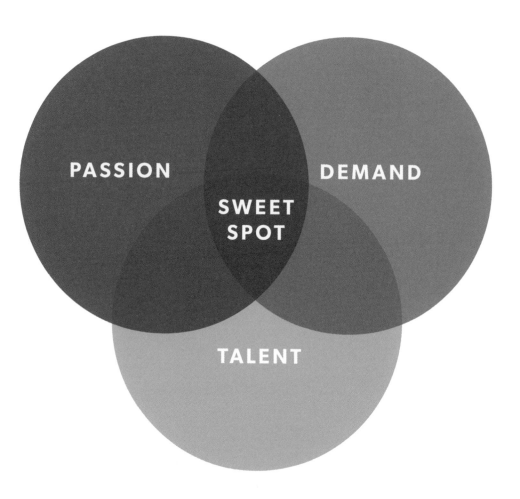

Everyone wants to find the sweet spot, the place where your talent, passion, and demand for your work all overlap. You'll get there, but it takes time and a lot of trial and error. Once you find the sweet spot, continue to readjust to stay there!

TALENT - What you're good at.
PASSION - That drive you've got to always learn, do better, work harder.
DEMAND - What people will pay for.

If only two of these overlaps, you may find yourself frustrated or unfulfilled. The magic happens when all three overlap.

BUCKET LIST PROJECTS

Write down the projects you dream about!

-
-
-
-
-
-
-
-
-
-
-
-
-
-
-

1 YEAR GOALS

-
-
-
-
-
-
-
-

1 YEAR GOALS	
•	•
•	•
•	•
•	•
•	•
•	•
•	•
•	•

2 YEAR GOALS

-
-
-
-
-
-
-
-

5 YEAR GOALS

-
-
-
-
-
-
-
-

CONTINUED EDUCATION

That fire inside you as an entrepreneur is what makes you always want to do better, work smarter, and dream bigger. That fire is what makes you successful, and you have to feed the fire by continuing to learn. Books, online courses, workshops, take them all! Here are a few of my go-to learning resources:

LOCAL WORKSHOPS - Take a letterpress, ceramics, or photography class! Learning a new skill may spark some creatives juices or help you bring a new perspective to the work you already do. It also helps prevent burn-out.

LYNDA - Learn software and business skills through these online courses.

YOUTUBE® TUTORIALS - Honestly, does anyone read manuals anymore?

SKILLSHARE - I love to see how other people work, so I have taken classes about things I already know and feel confident in, just to see if I can learn something new. I always do! I even teach a class on Skillshare® about lettering with Adobe® Illustrator®.

ADOBE® BEHANCE® LIVE - Another awesome way to see other people working, and keep you entertained! The live contests challenge you and are a fun way to get involved.

LIBRARIES - Hopefully you haven't forgotten that libraries exist! I love visiting my local library and taking out books about business! If I end up really loving the book, I will often buy a copy for my bookshelf.

BOOKSTORES & COFFEE SHOPS - Looking through art books gets me totally fired up. Get off the computer and get inspired looking through vintage books!

CHALLENGES - Get involved in online challenges—it'll help you grow your craft, hold you accountable, and give you a way to infuse your style, share your work and connect with others. Find a specific challenge for your industry by doing a quick online or social media search.

WE ARE *used to* LOOKING *outward* FOR INSPIRATION — THE *entirety* OF THE *internet* SITS THERE *waiting* FOR *you to* EXPLORE, BE IT SOCIAL *media,* IMAGE *search,* DESIGN *inspiration* SITES, AND *numerous* OTHER PLACES YOU CAN GO AND "*get inspired.*" HOWEVER, *the truth* IS THAT *real inspiration comes from yourself.* THE *best* WAY TO GET *inspired* IS TO MAKE STUFF. *make anything.* MAKE *bad* THINGS. MAKE *silly* THINGS. MAKE WORK YOU WOULD *never* SHOW ANYONE ELSE. IT DOES NOT *matter,* AS *long* AS YOU *are* MAKING, BECAUSE THAT *will provide you* WITH *infinite inspiration.* MAKING *makes ideas.*

MITCH GOLDSTEIN

DESIGNER & EDUCATOR | MITCHGOLDSTEIN.COM | @MGOLDST

final thoughts

NOTES and TAKEAWAYS

You did it! You finished the book. You're serious about your business and you're making waves! You're crushing it and I'm rooting for you!

NOTES

NOTES

SYSTEMS

17 HATS
ACUITY SCHEDULING™
AIRTABLE®
ASANA®
BASECAMP™
BONSAI®
DUBSABO
EVERNOTE®
GOOGLE DRIVE™
MONDAY™
SLACK
TODOIST®

EMAIL

BOOMERANG
COVERTKIT
MAILBOOST FOR GMAIL®
MAILCHIMP®
NEWTON™ APP
POLYMAIL®

MONEY

FRESHBOOKS®
HARVEST
HONEYBOOK®
OUTRIGHT BOOKKEEPING
QUICKBOOKS ONLINE
SQUARE™
WAVE
XERO™

PRODUCT BASED

SHIPSTATION®
TRADESHOW BOOTCAMP®

WELLNESS

INSIGHT TIMER
YOGA W/ ADRIENE

INSPIRATION

BEHANCE®
COLOURLOVERS™
CUBICLE REFUGEE
DESIGNSPIRATION®
DRIBBBLE™
LOVELY PACKAGE
MEDIUM
PINTEREST®
SITE INSPIRE
THE BEST DESIGNS

WEB

ELEMENTOR™
ETSY
GOOGLE™ KEYWORD PLANNER
GO LIVE HQ
TREE HOUSE
SHOPIFY™
SHOWIT
SQUARESPACE®
WORDPRESS®
WP ENGINE
YOAST® SEO

PRINTING

FRONTIER LABEL™
GEORGETTE
LUMI
MAMA'S SAUCE
MOO®
NEWSPAPER CLUB
PACKLANE®
PAPER CHASE PRESS
PARABO PRESS™
PRINTSFUL

SOCIAL MEDIA

AFTERLIGHT®
BUFFER
LATER APP
LINK TREE™
VSCO®

VISIT ILANAGRIFFO.COM/MINDYOURBUSINESS/RESOURCES FOR MORE

DESIGN TOOLS

ADOBE® CREATIVE CLOUD®
CREATIVE MARKET®
CSS VIEWER
DEATH TO STOCK PHOTO™
GRAPHIC BURGER
LOGOCORE
PIXEDEN
SCANNER PRO
THE NOUN PROJECT
WORDMARK

PODCASTS

BEING BOSS
BUILDING A STORYBRAND
GARYVEE
GIRLBOSS RADIO
GOAL DIGGER PODCAST
JEN GOTCH IS OK...SOMETIMES
PROOF TO PRODUCT
SMART PASSIVE INCOME

VIDEO

GARYVEE
MARIE*TV*
TED TALKS

LEARNING

LYNDA.COM®
SKILLSHARE.COM®

SCARY STUFF

BIZINSURE.COM®
FREELANCERSUNION.ORG®
FRIENDDA.ORG
IRS.GOV/BUSINESSES
LEGALZOOM.COM®
MILE IQ™
SBA.GOV

GROUPS

AIGA
BEING BOSS
CREATIVE LADY COLLECTIVE
SCORE
THE IMPERFECT BOSS
THE RISING TIDE SOCIETY
THINK CREATIVE COLLECTIVE

BOOKS

ART INC. *By Lisa Congdon and Meg Mateo Ilasco*
BIG MAGIC *By Elizabeth Gilbert*
CREATIVE INC. *By Ed Catmull and Amy Wallace*
CRUSHING IT / CRUSH IT *By Gary Vaynerchuk*
ESSENTIALISM *By James Latham*
GOOD TO GREAT *By Jim Collins*
GRAPHIC ARTISTS GUILD HANDBOOK *By Artists Guild Graphic*
PURPLE COW *By Seth Godin*
START WITH WHY *By Simon Sinek*
STEAL LIKE AN ARTIST *By Austin Kleon*
THE FOUR HOUR WORK WEEK *By Timothy Ferriss*
THE ONE THING *By Gary Keller and Jay Papasan*
THE POMODORO TECHNIQUE *By Francesco Cirillo*
THE TOTAL MONEY MAKEOVER *By Dave Ramsey*
THE WAR OF ART *By Steven Pressfield*
YOU ARE A BADASS *By Jen Sincero*

VISIT ILANAGRIFFO.COM/MINDYOURBUSINESS/RESOURCES FOR MORE

CREDITS

Chapter 1
Guillebeau, Chris. *The $100 Startup.* New York: Currency, 2012.

Chapter 4
Hill, Napoleon. *The Law of Success.* New York: Tarcher Perigee, 2008.

Chapter 7
Cirillo, Francesco. *The Pomodoro Technique.* New York: Random House Inc., 2018.

Chapter 8
Monteiro, Mike. F*ck You, Pay Me. Talk hosted by Typekit at Creative Mornings seminar, San Fransisco, CA March 2011.

ABOUT THE AUTHOR

Ilana Griffo is a graphic designer and illustrator with typographic tendencies. As a freelance designer and illustrator, her job is to translate her clients' stories into a visual experience. Her personality and work process can be described as fast-paced and bursting with creative energy.

Ilana launched her business as a side hustle, first designing a stationery line, *Sugar & Type* which includes the *Rule the World Planner*, a weekly planner designed for creative go-getters. After leaving her full-time job as an art director in 2015, she quickly grew her side hustle into a six-figure design studio. Her work has been featured on Buzzfeed™, as well as other gems across the internet, and in various print publications. Ilana is approachable, honest, and sassy; she understands the challenges creative business owners face and is passionate about helping them to achieve their goals and reach their professional dreams.

In addition to serving her own clients, Ilana has served as a Program Director for the upstate New York chapter of AIGA (the American Institute of Graphic Arts) and embraces opportunities to connect with fellow creatives in person and through social media. She teaches workshops throughout upstate New York and has taught as an adjunct instructor at the Rochester Institute of Technology.

Ilana balances sass with sweet; she strongly believes in eating dessert first and always. She lives in Rochester, New York with her bike enthusiast husband, Gregg, son Heath, and their dog, Dizzy.

SAY HI!

@ILANAGRIFFO
ILANAGRIFFO.COM

#MINDYOURBIZBOOK